LifeLight

"In Him was life, and that life was the light of men." John 1:4

Acts, Part 1

—

LEADERS GUIDE

CONCORDIA PUBLISHING HOUSE · SAINT LOUIS

Fresh ink glistens by lamplight. A disciple dips his reed pen and writes another line: "But Stephen, full of the Holy Spirit, looked up to heaven and saw the glory of God, and Jesus standing at the right hand of God" (Acts 7:55). The Book of Acts records God's glorious actions among the first believers. It reveals the light of Christ, which spread by speech and scroll from Jerusalem down to our day.

Copyright © 1993, 2004 by Concordia Publishing House
3558 S. Jefferson Avenue
St. Louis, MO 63118-3968

Earl H. Gaulke, editor

Revised from material prepared by Edward A. Westcott and Donna Streufert

Denise Muhly and Lawrence Schmidt, field test coordinators, St Peter Lutheran Church, Lodi, California

This publication may be available in braille, in large print, or on cassette tape for the visually impaired. Please allow 8 to 12 weeks for delivery. Write to the Library for the Blind, 1333 S. Kirkwood Road, St. Louis, MO 63122-7295; call 1-800-433-3954, ext. 1322; or e-mail to blind.library@lcms.org.

Manufactured in the U.S.A.

Cover illustration: Chris Ellison

Contents

Introduction

Welcome to LifeLight

A special pleasure is in store for you. You will be instrumental in leading your brothers and sisters in Christ closer to Him who is our life and light (John 1:4). You will have the pleasure of seeing fellow Christians discover new insights and rediscover old ones as they open the Scriptures and dig deep into them, perhaps deeper than they have ever dug before. More than that, you will have the pleasure of sharing in this wonderful study.

LifeLight—An In-depth Study

LifeLight is a series of in-depth Bible studies. The goal of LifeLight is that through a regular program of in-depth personal and group study of Scripture, more and more Christian adults may grow in their personal faith in Jesus Christ, enjoy fellowship with the members of His body, and reach out in love to others in witness and service.

In-depth means that this Bible study includes the following four components: individual daily home study; discussion in a small group; a lecture presentation on the Scripture portion under study; and an enhancement of the week's material (through reading the enrichment magazine).

LifeLight Participants

LifeLight participants are adults who desire a deeper study of the Scriptures than is available in the typical Sunday morning adult Bible class. (Mid-to-older teens might also be LifeLight participants.) While LifeLight does not assume an existing knowledge of the Bible or special experience or skills in Bible study, it does assume a level of commitment that will bring participants to each of the nine weekly assemblies having read the assigned readings and attempted to answer the study questions. Daily reading and study will require from 15 to 30 minutes for the five days preceding the LifeLight assembly. The day following the assembly will be spent reviewing the previous week's study by going over the completed study leaflet and the enrichment magazine.

LifeLight Leadership

While the in-depth process used by LifeLight begins with individual study and cannot achieve its aims without this individual effort, it cannot be completed by individual study alone. Therefore, trained leaders are necessary. You fill one or perhaps more of the important roles described below.

The Director

This person oversees the LifeLight program in a local center (which may be a congregation or a center operated by several neighboring congregations). The director

- serves as the parish LifeLight overall coordinator and leader;
- coordinates the scheduling of the LifeLight program;
- orders materials;
- convenes LifeLight leadership team meetings;
- develops publicity materials;
- recruits participants;
- maintains records and budgeting;
- assigns, with the leadership team, participants to small discussion groups;
- makes arrangements for facilities;
- communicates outreach opportunities to small-group leaders and to congregational boards;
- follows up on participants who leave the program.

The Assistant Director *(optional)*

This person may assist the director. Duties listed for the director may be assigned to the assistant director as mutually agreeable.

The Lecture Leader

This person prepares and delivers the lecture at the weekly assembly. **(Lesson material for the lecture leader begins on p. 9.)** The lecture leader

- prepares and presents the Bible study lecture to the large group;

- prepares worship activities (devotional thought, hymn, prayer), using resources in the study leaflet and leaders guide and possibly other outside sources;

- helps the small-group discussion leaders to grow in understanding the content of the lessons;

- encourages prayer at weekly leadership-team and discussion-leaders equipping meetings.

The Small-Group Coordinator *(optional; the director may fill this role)*

This person supervises and coordinates the work of the small-group discussion leaders. The small-group coordinator

- recruits with the leadership team the small-group discussion leaders;

- trains or arranges for training of the discussion leaders;

- assists the director and discussion leaders in follow-up and outreach;

- encourages the discussion leaders to contact absent group members;

- participates in the weekly leadership-team and discussion-leaders equipping meetings;

- provides ongoing training and support as needed.

The Small-Group Discussion Leaders

These people guide and facilitate discussion of LifeLight participants in the small groups. **(Lesson material for the small-group leaders begins on p. 49.)** There should be one discussion leader for every group of no more than 12 participants. The small-group discussion leaders are, perhaps, those individuals who are most important to the success of the program. They should, therefore, be chosen with special care and be equipped with skills needed to guide discussion and to foster a caring fellowship within the group. These discussion leaders

- prepare each week for the small-group discussion by using the study leaflet and small-group leaders guide section for that session **(see p. 49)**;

- read the enrichment magazine as a study supplement;

- guide and facilitate discussion in their small group;

- encourage and assist the discussion group in prayer;

- foster fellowship and mutual care within the discussion group;

- attend weekly discussion leaders training meetings.

Leadership Training

LifeLight leaders will meet weekly to review the previous week's work and plan the coming week. At this session, leaders can address concerns and prepare for the coming session. LifeLight is a 1½-hour program with no possibility for it to be taught in the one hour typically available on Sunday mornings. Some congregations, however, may want to use the Sunday morning Bible study hour for LifeLight preparation and leadership training. In such a meeting, the lecture leader and/or small-group coordinator may lead the discussion leaders through the coming week's lesson, reserving 5 or 10 minutes for problem solving or other group concerns.

While it requires intense effort, LifeLight has proven to bring great benefit to LifeLight participants. The effort put into this program, both by leaders and by participants, will be rewarding and profitable.

The LifeLight Weekly Schedule

Here is how LifeLight will work week by week:

1. Before session 1, each participant will receive the study leaflet for session 1 and the enrichment magazine for the course. The study leaflet contains worship resources (for use both in individual daily study and at the opening of the following week's assembly) and readings and study questions for five days. Challenge questions will lead those participants who have the time and desire a greater challenge into even deeper levels of study.

2. After the five days of individual study at home, participants will gather for a weekly assembly of all LifeLight participants. The assembly will begin with a brief period of worship (5 minutes). Participants will then join their assigned small discussion groups (of 12 or fewer, who will remain the same throughout the course), where they will go over the week's

study questions together (55 minutes). Assembling together once again, participants will listen to a lecture presentation on the readings they have studied in the previous week and discussed in their small groups (20 minutes). After the lecture presentation, the director or another leader will distribute the study leaflet for the following week. Closing announcements and other necessary business may take another five minutes before dismissal.

In some places some small groups will not join the weekly assembly because of scheduling or other reasons. Such groups may meet at another time and place (perhaps in the home of one of the small group's members). They will follow the same schedule, but they may use the cassette tape to listen to the week's lecture presentation. The discussion leader will obtain the tape and leaflets from the director. A cassette tape version of the lecture is available for purchase from CPH (see your catalog). Or a congregation may record the lecture given by the lecture leader at the weekly assembly and duplicate it for use by other groups meeting later in the week.

3. On the day following the assembly, participants will review the preceding week's work by rereading the study leaflet they completed (and that they perhaps supplemented or corrected during the discussion in their small group) and by reading appropriate articles in the enrichment magazine.

Then the LifeLight weekly study process will begin all over again!

Recommended Study Resources for Acts

Bruce, F. F. *The Acts of the Apostles: The Greek Text with Introduction and Commentary*, 2nd ed. Grand Rapids, MI: Eerdmans, 1952; revised and enlarged, 1990. A verse-by-verse exposition on the basis of the Greek text; helpful introductory articles.

Bruce, F. F. *The Book of the Acts* (NICNT). Grand Rapids, MI: Eerdmans, 1953; revised and enlarged, 1988. Carefully explores each event recorded in the Book of Acts. A valuable resource.

Concordia Self-Study Bible, New International Version. St. Louis: Concordia Publishing House, 1986. Interpretive notes on each page form a running commentary of the text. The book includes cross-references, a 35,000-word concordance, full-color maps, charts, and timelines.

Harrison, Everett F. *Acts: The Expanding Church*. Chicago: Moody, 1976. A very helpful exposition written in a simple style.

Lenski, R. C. H. *The Interpretation of the Acts of the Apostles*. Columbus, OH: The Wartburg Press, 1944. An older but basically reliable commentary by a Lutheran scholar.

Marshall, I. Howard. *The Acts of the Apostles* (TNTC). Grand Rapids, MI: Eerdmans, 1980. A modern commentary on Acts by a careful scholar; contains some mildly critical overtones.

Roehrs, Walter R., and Martin H. Franzmann. *Concordia Self-Study Commentary*. St. Louis: Concordia Publishing House, 1979. An invaluable one-volume commentary on the Bible.

Every Voice a Song: Pipe Organ Accompaniment for 180 Hymns and Liturgy. St. Louis: Concordia Publishing House (order no. 99-1565). Use this music CD for worship hymn accompaniment.

The Church Is Prepared for Pentecost

Acts 1

Preparing for the Session

Central Focus

As we begin this study of Acts, we are introduced to its author, Luke; we hear Jesus' final instructions to His disciples before He ascends into heaven; and we observe the manner by which the ranks of the 12 apostles are restored after the defection of Judas.

Objectives

That participants, led by the Holy Spirit, will

1. understand the purpose of this book and its relationship to Luke's Gospel;

2. realize the importance of proclaiming the Gospel to the world as the central task of Christians and the reason why the world continues to exist;

3. desire to make sharing the Gospel with others a primary goal of their lives;

4. seek opportunities to pray and worship together with fellow Christians as a means of strengthening themselves as witnesses for Jesus.

Note for the small-group leaders: Lesson notes and other materials you will need begin on page 51.

Session Plan

Worship

Begin the session with the hymn printed in the study leaflet and the devotion below. Hymn accompaniments are available in denominational hymnals, such as *Lutheran Worship* (refer to hymnal index). Note: Concordia Publishing House has available *Every Voice a Song*, a 9-CD set of organ accompaniments for 180 hymns and liturgy. All the initial worship hymns in the LifeLight courses are included in this resource. It's especially helpful for mission congregations and small parishes. See the list of study resources on page 7.

Devotion

Do you like to read history?

This book of Christian history portrays a subject important to us. How did—and does—the Good News about Jesus get out into the world? How did—and does—the church grow? How did—and do—Christians grow in their faith? How does the Holy Spirit work through people, and how do people work through the Holy Spirit?

Furthermore, this history is the work of an inspired—and inspiring—writer. Some of what he tells us was the result of careful research and of interviewing witnesses. Some of it the writer experienced firsthand. All of what he wrote was inspired by the Holy Spirit, who is Himself the primary actor in this history.

All in all, we're going to find that this history is not boring or irrelevant, but fascinating and faith building. This is history we can all study with eagerness!

Lecture Presentation

1 Introduction to Acts

We are beginning the study of one of the most fascinating and beautiful books in the Bible. Many people have spent years futilely searching for errors in the great amount of geographical and historical data and the 110 names of persons contained in the book.

More important than its beauty of style and historical accuracy, even in details, is the wealth of important Christian teachings found in Acts. Acts is a beautiful mirror in which we can clearly see the great scriptural truth that we are justified (saved) by faith alone—and how this "Gospel," this "Good News," spread throughout the ancient world.

Close with the prayer in the study leaflet.

2 Author, Date, and Purpose

Although Luke never mentions himself as the writer of either his Gospel or Acts, the fact that he wrote both is solidly attested to by ancient tradition. All we really know about his background is that he bore a Gentile name and was probably a native of Antioch. In Colossians 4:14 Paul calls Luke "the doctor."

The dates when Luke wrote his Gospel and Acts have been the subject of much argument and debate. Most scholars, however, believe that he wrote shortly after Paul's execution in A.D. 66 and before the destruction of Jerusalem in A.D. 70.

For Luke the writing of Acts was a joyous sequel to the writing of his Gospel. He wrote both books to one person named Theophilus with whom Luke appears to have developed a close friendship during his long stay in Rome. (Since "Theophilus" in Greek means "lover of God," some think it is not a name at all, but a phrase describing the reader.) All we can gather about Theophilus is from Luke 1:3-4. "Most excellent Theophilus" indicates that Luke's friend was either a knight, held an official position of some sort, or was a person of great wealth and prominence.

More important, it is evident that Theophilus was interested in Christianity. The Gospel, therefore, had a missionary purpose—to win Luke's friend to faith in Christ. When the Spirit blessed Luke's purpose and his friend became a believer (note the omission of the title in Acts 1:1), Luke's desire to build up and nurture that new faith resulted in his writing for Theophilus the book called Acts.

The original purposes the Spirit used to provide His church of all ages with these two inspired records have not changed. We need to recognize that and allow the Spirit to accomplish the original purpose of Acts in us as we study privately and together. To paraphrase Peter (1 Peter 2:2), no matter how long we've been in the faith, let's become like newborn babies, craving the spiritual milk of this book, so that through this study the Spirit can give us a new and joyous understanding of what it means to belong to Him Who loved us and gave Himself for us that we might be His "new creation!" (2 Corinthians 5:17)

3 Brief Overview

Luke begins this book where he left off in his Gospel. He then proceeds to provide the basic history of the beginning, spread, and growth of Christianity during the 30 years immediately following the death, resurrection, and ascension of Christ. The key verse is 1:8.

The rest of the book follows the outline of the last part of that verse, graphically picturing the witness in "Jerusalem" (1:1–8:4), the witness in "Judea and Samaria" (8:5–12:25) and the witness "to the ends of the earth" (13–28). While there are 110 individuals named throughout the book, the first 12 chapters highlight the words and activities of Peter, and the last 16 chapters do the same for Paul. And, finally, Acts serves as the link between the four Gospels and all the letters that make up the rest of the New Testament.

4 Bridge between Luke's Gospel and Acts (1:1–5)

The opening five verses summarize the entire book. Luke brings to mind all that he had written about the deeds and the teachings of Jesus up to the time of the ascension. He reintroduces us to the apostles Jesus selected. He recalls the 40 days in which Jesus gave proof of His resurrection and spoke of the things of the kingdom. He repeats the command (Luke 24:49) that the apostles must not leave Jerusalem, for in a few days the promise of the coming of the Spirit would be fulfilled.

5 Ascension of Christ (1:6–11)

Luke begins with an overlap, expanding the brief account of the ascension in his Gospel (24:50–53) with important additional information. Verse 6 places us at the ascension. We learn from verse 12 that this was on the Mount of Olives, the base of which was about three-fourths of a mile—the "Sabbath day's walk"—from Jerusalem. The actual site was probably on the eastern slope of the mount, overlooking Jerusalem.

Apparently, the apostles had been discussing the subject of the question they now blurted out. What they were really asking is not important. What is important is Jesus' answer in verses 7–8. In these pivotal words,

Christ gives the apostles and us a much-needed warning: Don't spend energy and time on issues and subjects that will only distract and deter us from our God-given mission. And, especially, don't get trapped into endless discussions of issues that are none of our business, for which the Lord has not given us answers.

Earlier Christ had clearly and unmistakably stated the exclusive purpose of the final era of this world's history with the words of Matthew 24:14: "And this gospel of the kingdom will be preached in the whole world as a testimony to all nations, and *then the end will come.*" Now Christ reemphasizes that great truth and places the responsibility for carrying out that purpose squarely on the shoulders of the apostles *and the believers who would follow them.* This is why He is not taking them with Him. One more job remained to be done before the end comes, and He needed them to accomplish it.

"Be My witnesses." While we apply the word *witness* to ourselves, the apostles were witnesses as no others were or could ever be. How grateful we are that their witness did not die with them, but that the Holy Spirit inspired them to leave a written account of it. Because of this we can speak with the same certainty as if we were indeed eyewitnesses.

With the words in verse 8, "in Jerusalem, and in all Judea and Samaria, and to the ends of the earth," Christ gives Luke his outline for writing this book and, more important, details the exact plan or method the apostles—and we too—are to use in being witnesses. Start where you live, then move out in ever-widening circles until all nations have heard of God's love for them in Christ. But in moving out never, never overlook those among whom you are living. Christ shatters the "over there" mission mentality that has stalled the growth of Christianity in our country. We don't live where we live or work where we work by accident. That's where Christ has placed us so that through us He can reach those who don't as yet know and love Him as we do.

With hands raised in blessing, Christ now triumphantly closes His earthly ministry. The apostles know they will not see Him physically on earth again. As they watch, straining their eyes to see Him as long as they can, a cloud folds Him in and He is gone from their sight.

Truly, in every way, Christ's moment of triumph is our assurance that all that the Father had sent Him to do

was accomplished. The wall of separation was forever broken down. Forgiveness was real, for He had paid the price for every sin, enduring the torment of the damned in their place, reconciling the entire human race to His Father. And, by His resurrection, heaven was again opened to all who by faith accepted Him as their Lord and Savior.

There are at least two other critically important truths flowing out of Christ's ascension that, when understood, can bring a new excitement and sharper focus to our Christian living. The first of these truths is eloquently expressed by the apostle Paul in Ephesians 1:22–23: "And God placed all things under His feet and appointed Him to be head over everything *for the church,* which is His body, the fullness of Him who fills everything in every way."

"All things . . . everything . . . for the church!" Everything, on a worldwide and on a personal level, is under Christ's control and direction, and—even when we don't always see or understand how—is directly related to the single reason for the continuation of time and history—"for the church."

(Galatians 2:20) "I have been crucified with Christ and I no longer live, but Christ lives in me" is Paul's way of stating the second great truth flowing out of Christ's ascension. Christ ascended so that He might become visible in every nation and language and culture of the world. How? Through the lives and words of those in whom He has taken up residence.

This is why He has scattered His believers throughout every nation of the world. This is why we live where we live and work where we work—"for the church!" Christ sets events in motion and then steps back, counting on us in whom He lives to make Him visible to that unbelieving neighbor or co-worker.

This great truth can bring an excitement and a new purpose and vision into our lives. Colossians 4:5 tells us to "make the most of every opportunity." If only every Christian understood and lived this great truth, the world would again be turned upside down for Christ!

6 Awaiting the Baptism of the Holy Spirit

A. Prayer and Worship (1:12–14)

Responding to the angels' prompting, the apostles

returned to Jerusalem with great joy (Luke 24:52). Remembering Jesus' words that they were to wait for the gift of the Holy Spirit, they made an upper room somewhere in Jerusalem their headquarters. Whenever they met together, one in heart and mind, they joined together in worship and prayer.

Luke introduced the apostles to Theophilus in verse 1, but now he wants him to know by name those who had witnessed the ascension of Jesus. He is also setting the scene for the replacement of Judas. At the same time, Luke expands the group that gathered together each day. He adds the women, probably those at the crucifixion and the resurrection. The only name mentioned is Mary, Jesus' mother, who was in John's care. Without comment or explanation Jesus' brothers also are listed as part of the worshiping and praying group. Named as unbelievers by John (7:5), it is quite probable that the resurrection of Jesus brought them to faith.

B. Choosing Judas's Successor (1:15–26)

The fact that the number of apostles must be 12 according to the original choosing of Jesus appears to have been taken for granted. That this was necessary in order to match the 12 patriarchs, the 12 tribes of Israel, and the 12 thrones awaiting them to judge these 12 tribes was undoubtedly also the basis for this decision.

However, the Eleven did not act by themselves but called together as large a number of male believers as possible, somewhere around 120. Peter acted as chairman of this first congregational meeting. He introduced the purpose of the meeting with as clear a definition of verbal inspiration as found anywhere in Scripture (v. 16) "which the Holy Spirit spoke long ago through the mouth of David." He then proceeded to give a brief summary of the recent events surrounding Judas and the eternal consequences of his action. He quoted Psalm 69:25 and 109:8 in support of the action they were about to take. And finally, Peter stated the qualifications that the man who was to replace Judas must have. In order to be numbered with the Twelve and have credibility as a primary witness, the one chosen must have been with those who were around Jesus from the time John was baptizing up to, but not including, the ascension.

Two men qualified—Joseph called Barsabbas and Matthias. The choice between the two was entrusted to

Jesus through prayer. This is the only time the New Testament records the church using the Old Testament method of casting lots. Probably two markers, each with one name written on it, were placed into some sort of a vessel. This was then shaken so hard that one marker flew out. Or a name was drawn out. In this way Christ chose Matthias, and the 11 became 12 again.

All this by way of introduction. The scene is set. We can sense the tension and excitement that must have filled the room every time they came together. Will the Holy Spirit come today? In what way? How will we know? What will be the result?

Concluding Activities

Close with a brief prayer, perhaps thanking God for the Book of Acts and asking Him to bless your study of it. Then make any necessary announcements and distribute study leaflet 2 and the enrichment magazines. Encourage participants to read the magazine for further enrichment and background to accompany their study.

The Church Is Empowered by the Holy Spirit

Acts 2:1–41

Preparing for the Session

Central Focus

On Pentecost Day the Holy Spirit came upon Jesus' followers, as Jesus had promised and as Joel and John the Baptist had prophesied, drawing a large crowd from many nations around them. Peter proclaimed the Gospel to this crowd by an inspired sermon, and the result was that 3,000 people were moved by the Spirit to repentance and to faith in Jesus as the Messiah.

Objectives

That participants, led by the Holy Spirit, will

1. realize that the events of Pentecost Day were in fulfillment of prophecy and of Jesus' promise;

2. understand that God gives the gift of the Holy Spirit to all believers through Holy Baptism;

3. become more aware of and confident in the Holy Spirit's presence in them;

4. desire to share the Gospel with others;

5. by repentance and faith reclaim the baptismal gifts each day and begin again to live a new life of holiness and righteousness by the Spirit's power.

Note for small-group leaders: Lesson notes and other materials you will need begin on page 53.

Session Plan

Worship

Begin the session with the hymn printed in the study leaflet and the devotion below. Hymn accompaniments are available in denominational hymnals, such as *Lutheran Worship* (refer to hymnal index). Note: Concordia Publishing House has available *Every Voice a Song,* a 9-CD set of organ accompaniments for 180 hymns and liturgy. All the initial worship hymns in the LifeLight courses are included in this resource. It's especially helpful for mission congregations and small parishes. See the list of study resources on page 7.

Devotion

When people who speak different languages converse, they usually make use of translators or interpreters. The process of speaking through a translator can be tedious and difficult. In our lesson this week, we see how God Himself served as a translator, miraculously translating the words of Christians into many different languages on Pentecost Day. By this miracle God showed that the Gospel was for people of all nations and languages.

Today God is still using Christians to speak the Gospel to people of many different languages. Christians learn the languages of the people they are addressing or perhaps use human interpreters. But what God, on Pentecost, miraculously showed would happen is happening—people of many languages are hearing the Gospel in their own native tongue.

And the ultimate result of all this? John's vision of heaven: (Revelation 7:9–10) "After this I looked and there before me was a great multitude that no one could count, from every nation, tribe, people and language, standing before the throne and in front of the Lamb. They were wearing white robes and were holding palm branches in their hands. And they cried out in a loud voice: 'Salvation belongs to our God, who sits on the throne, and to the Lamb.'"

Close with the prayer in the study leaflet.

Lecture Presentation

1 Introduction

How were 12 men to evangelize the world of all time? How were they to storm Satan's citadel and reach the ends of the earth and all generations of people until the end of time? How were they—fishermen, tax collectors, ordinary people—to establish the one holy Christian and apostolic church?

Not in and of themselves, that's for sure. That's why Christ ordered them to stay together and wait for (1:4) "the gift My Father promised." (1:5) "In a few days," He told them, "you will be baptized with the Holy Spirit" and (1:8) "you will receive power" from Him. In advance and in His own way, the Savior defined for the apostles the miracle of Pentecost, dealing directly with the feelings of helplessness and inadequacy that must have begun to overwhelm them as they listened to Him describe their lives after He would leave them.

And Pentecost tells us that we don't go it alone. The same power and gifts that changed the apostles into courageous ambassadors for Christ are ours today. The Holy Spirit will give us the right moment, the right words, and the courage to tell the mystery of Christ as clearly as we should. He enables us to be wise in the way we act toward outsiders and helps us to make the most of every opportunity. He keeps our conversation always full of grace and meaningful when we are asked (1 Peter 3:15) "to give the reason for the hope that you have." Even when we are at a loss for words, He will (Luke 12:11–12) "teach you at that time what you should say."

2 The Holy Spirit Comes (2:1–4a)

Pentecost was the name of one of the three annual Jewish feasts for which all males of Israel were required to travel to the temple in Jerusalem (Exodus 23:14–19). A one-day Jewish harvest festival that celebrated the completion of the harvest, it was also called the Feast of Weeks or the Feast of Harvest. Literally, the name *Pentecost* means "50th day," coming on the 50th day after the Feast of the Passover.

While all this is informative and interesting, what is really important is the fact that the Lord chose a day for the outpouring of the Holy Spirit and the beginning of the Christian church when the city of Jerusalem was literally teeming with people from all over the Mediterranean world. On that day, shortly before nine in the morning, the apostles and the other believers were meeting together for prayer and discussion.

Verse 2—At the moment of the miracle, the entire assembly was sitting on the floor listening to one of the apostles. Suddenly, without warning, a loud roar like a violent wind sounded in the sky, but there was no wind. Not a leaf on a tree moved. But the sound grew in inten-

sity and moved from the sky through the city to the house where the believers were gathered. It does not take much imagination to guess the reaction throughout the city.

Inside the building the believers were on their feet. The "coming" was happening! Undoubtedly they sensed the power in the volume of the sound that surrounded them. And before they could catch their breath, the second miraculous sign happened.

Verse 3—A large ball of fire that wasn't fire entered the room and divided into individual tongues of flame that rested briefly on the head of everyone in the room—men, women, and children. These firelike tongues are plainly a fulfillment of the prophecy that John the Baptist had made—that the Messiah would baptize His followers with the Holy Spirit and with fire (Matthew 3:11)—and are a clear symbol of the divine presence of the Holy Spirit.

The sound roared indiscriminately through the whole house, but these tongues sat upon each individual in the room. The different Greek words Luke uses here and in verses 6 and 8 clearly indicate that Luke here means "on each single one," not a single person being excepted, men, women, old, young. The Holy Spirit fills every single believer in the church and equips all for the glorious task of making God's love in Christ known to all people everywhere.

In that sense Pentecost goes on and on and on. No, there are no tongues that look like fire, no roaring sound, no flashing neon lights or rockets going off today—just the quiet miracle of Baptism through which He makes us His new creation. At that moment the Holy Spirit takes up residence in each of us and equips us to be His messengers to a world that, by and large, still sits in darkness and the shadow of death.

3 Evidence of the Spirit's Indwelling Presence (2:4b–13)

Verse 4—"All of them were filled with the Holy Spirit." This is the miracle. The signs are the visible evidence. Besides the roar of noise and the tongues of flame on each head, there was another sign that they "were filled with the Holy Spirit." They "began to speak in other tongues as the Spirit enabled them." The sound and the tongues of flame were external. But this miraculous speaking in a language other than their own was clearly proof that the Holy Spirit had entered each one. Every word of these foreign languages underscored God's purpose to spread the Gospel to every nation. This miracle is prophetic. It is the first full chord of that symphony of confession, testimony, prayer, and praise that was soon to come from the 6,170 languages of all the nations of today's world.

Meanwhile, outside the house in which all this was joyously happening, there was a great commotion. People were running through the streets, all being pulled toward the roar of sound as though by a magnet. Verse 6—Luke tells us that these were God-fearing Jews "from every nation under heaven." These were Jews who either lived and worked in foreign lands and were in Jerusalem for the feast days, or they had returned permanently to retire in Jerusalem. All of them, of course, knew and spoke Aramaic, because they obviously understood Peter when he preached. But they also knew well the language of the nation to which they would return or from which they had retired.

Verse 11—As the crowd gathered, they heard someone speaking "the wonders of God" in the language of the nation in which they lived or had lived. Since numerous languages were being spoken, it is no wonder that those in the crowd were bewildered, amazed, and perplexed. So the questions began to sweep through the crowd. Who were these people doing this? How could they do it? Apparently some in the crowd knew the disciples and quickly supplied the information. The reaction was one of astonishment. All from Galilee! None from the countries or nations whose language they were speaking! But this still did not answer the question of how these Galileans could do this or why they were doing it.

Verse 12—The majority of the large crowd appeared to be sensible and willing to wait for someone to give them answers to their questions. A few laughingly pointed their fingers and cynically shrugged the whole thing off with the words "They have had too much wine." Sound familiar?

4 The First Sermon of the Christian Era (2:14–36)

Far more impressive a sign of the Spirit's presence than the roaring noise were the tongues of flame and the speaking in foreign languages. The 12 apostles stepped to the front of the rest of the disciples. One of them, an ordinary fisherman named Peter, took one more step forward and, without preparation, boldly and clearly delivered a masterful sermon to this great assembly of thousands. (Luke 12:12) "For the Holy Spirit will teach you at that time what you should say."

Is there any reason why the Holy Spirit cannot and will not do the same for us today when we are suddenly given the opportunity to tell someone about the faith and hope within us? Has not this same Spirit been living in us since our Baptism? The major reason why so many of us live our lives completely unaware of this exciting truth is that we rarely, if ever, think or talk about it.

The apostle Paul loved to describe the Christian as one in whom Christ lives (Galatians 2:20), one whose body is the temple of the Holy Spirit (1 Corinthians 6:19). It's not too late to make these exciting truths a part of our thinking and our discussions. Becoming aware of the Spirit's presence and His power within us could turn the world upside down for Christ!

Back to the scene before us. Peter addressed his audience with authority. He asked the crowd to give him their undivided attention. If the Holy Spirit was going to reach into their hearts, He would do so through their ears (Romans 10:14, 17).

Peter then defused their allegation with two short sentences. Verse 15—"These men are not drunk, as you suppose. It's only nine in the morning!" The Jews drank wine only when they ate meat, which they ate only at the evening or main meal of the day. In the morning, especially on a festival day such as Pentecost, they ate only bread and that usually not until about 10 o'clock, after the morning sacrifice.

No, said Peter, what you hear is not the result of too much wine, but is the fulfillment of the Word of God spoken by the prophet Joel (about 870 B.C.).

Verses 17–18—"Your sons and daughters . . . young men . . . old men . . . both men and women." The Holy Spirit is given to all believers in this last age, irrespective of sex, age, or rank.

The purpose? Only one—that between now and "the coming of the great and glorious day of the Lord" (v. 20), people of all nations throughout the world will call on the name of the Lord and be saved (v. 21).

And now Peter, without hesitation or apology, recounts for his audience recent events still fresh in their minds about the man called "Jesus of Nazareth," their stubborn and blind rejection of Him, and, finally, the unexpected and blessed result of their actions—Law and Gospel. Verse 23—"By God's set purpose and foreknowledge" points to the complete and total inability of any human being to satisfy the justice of God, to remove the wall of separation, and cause God's face to shine favorably on us again (Isaiah 59:2).

And the proof that God's purpose had been accomplished? Verse 24—"But God raised Him from the dead, freeing Him from the agony of death, because it was impossible for death to keep its hold on Him." Powerful words! *You* "put Him to death"; "*God* raised Him from the dead." *You* "nail[ed] Him to the cross"; *God* "free[d] Him from the agony of death." Hammer blows of the Law. Balm and healing of the Gospel.

Verses 25–28—Then to validate the resurrection, Peter quoted the Scripture for a second time. This time the Holy Spirit doesn't use a lesser-known prophet such as Joel but the revered and respected King David. Verse 31—That David was not talking about himself but about the resurrection of Christ is obvious. Verse 32—Then Peter adds the clincher: "And we are all witnesses of the fact."

What brought you all here and what you witnessed when you came is further proof of this great truth. Verse 33—This Jesus is "exalted to the right hand of God, He has received from the Father the promised Holy Spirit and has poured out what you now see and hear."

It is important to note that this first apostolic message and all the ones that follow center in on the resurrection of Jesus. By this act the Father sealed Jesus as Lord and Christ. By this act the apostolic message and ours is given validity (1 Corinthians 15:12–34). Even more wonderful is the faith-strengthening and joyous fact that in our Baptism we were not only buried with Christ but have already experienced the resurrection with Him so that we now have the ability to "live a new life" for Him (Romans 6:4).

Verse 36—Peter's conclusion is powerful. Take Jesus, the Pentecost miracle, the prophecies of Joel and David, and what do they put beyond question? That "God has made this Jesus, whom you crucified, both Lord and Christ." Any other deduction is false to both the facts and the prophecies.

5 The Result of the Foolishness of Preaching (2:37–41)

Verse 37—The result? "They were cut to the heart." Repentance and acceptance of Jesus as Lord and Christ. Filled now with hurt over their former rejection of Jesus, they freely admit their guilt in the question "Brothers, what shall we do?"

Verse 38—"Repent and be baptized, every one of you, in the name of Jesus Christ for the forgiveness of your sins. And you will receive the gift of the Holy Spirit." Repentance involves an inner change of heart, a turning away from sin and unbelief to faith and cleansing in Christ.

"Be baptized." Baptism was important to John the Baptist and in the instructions of Jesus to the apostles (Matthew 28:19). Baptism is pure Gospel that gives the recipient grace and salvation from God through Christ. God does something for us in Baptism; we do nothing for Him. In the water and the Word, He acts on us and gives us the gifts of faith, forgiveness, and the Holy Spirit.

"For the forgiveness of your sins." How beautiful and sweet those words must have sounded in the people's ears! Again, this is one of those very special phrases that sets Christianity apart from every other religion and philosophy in the world. The Hebrew and Greek words simply mean "the sending away" of your sins. How far? Psalm 103:12 tells us "as far as the east is from the west, so far has He removed our transgressions from us."

Listen carefully, you who have problems with guilt. In Christ God removes sins from the sinner so as never to be found again. By His own statement there is one thing God cannot do—He cannot remember sins He has forgiven. Nor does guilt remain, for sin and guilt are one, and therefore both are gone. The believer will stand before the judgment seat of Christ clothed only in His righteousness; faultless. No other religion can offer personal freedom of such magnitude!

Verse 39—Forgiveness and the Holy Spirit cannot be separated from Baptism. Peter assured the people that this "promise is for you and your children" and then lifted their eyes to the other peoples and nations of the world who also are included in this promise: "and for all who are far off."

Verse 41—Finally, an astonishing statement: "Those who accepted his message were baptized, and about three thousand were added to their number that day." One sermon, and the Holy Spirit claimed about 3,000 converts! Not everyone in the crowd—but, still, 3,000! Think of 3,000 people coming to faith and to Baptism on that day, the very first day of what may be called the Christian church! On that day the great mother church of all Christendom was founded and started off with 3,000-plus members. No gimmicks, no audiovisuals. Just plain, straightforward, unembellished preaching of the Word of God, Law and Gospel. Do you think that maybe, just maybe, we could learn something from that?

Concluding Activities

Speak a brief prayer, perhaps asking the Holy Spirit to move us to respond to the Gospel with repentance and faith and with a greater desire to share that Gospel with others. Then make any necessary announcements. Ask whether participants are enjoying the enrichment magazines. Distribute study leaflet 3.

The Church Proclaims the Word with Great Boldness

Acts 2:42–4:31

Preparing for the Session

Central Focus

Boldly, the church—led by the apostles Peter and John—proclaims the Gospel about Jesus to the residents of Jerusalem and courageously defies the orders of the Sanhedrin to stop proclaiming this Gospel.

Objectives

That participants, led by the Holy Spirit, will

1. know that the courage to speak the Gospel boldly comes from the presence of the Holy Spirit within Christians;

2. desire to proclaim the Gospel more boldly in our world today;

3. devote themselves more consistently to the Gospel offered to us in Word and Sacrament;

4. be ready to speak boldly to others about God's love and grace for us in Jesus, the Savior.

Notes for the small-group leaders: Lesson notes and other materials you will need begin on page 56.

Session Plan

Worship

Begin the session with the hymn printed in the study leaflet and the devotion below. Hymn accompaniments are available in denominational hymnals, such as *Lutheran Worship* (refer to hymnal index). Note: Concordia Publishing House has available *Every Voice a Song,* a 9-CD set of organ accompaniments for 180 hymns and liturgy. All the initial worship hymns in the LifeLight courses are included in this resource. It's especially helpful for mission congregations and small parishes. See the list of study resources on page 7.

Devotion

Here's an old joke; maybe you've heard it. A man comes off the street into a church during worship. This man comes from a church background where people respond with "Amen" and "Hallelujah!" and "Praise the Lord!" when they feel moved to do so during worship. So, during the sermon the visitor shouts out "Amen!" Other worshipers turn and give an annoyed look at the visitor. A little later the visitor shouts once again, "Amen!" This time an usher approaches the visitor and reproves him with a "Shhhh." But the visitor will not be discouraged. Once again he shouts "Amen!" This time the usher tells the visitor: "Sir, you will have to be quiet." "But," protests the visitor, "I've got the Spirit." "Well," declares the usher, "you didn't get Him here!"

Perhaps we don't think worshipers ought to shout such outbursts during worship, either, preferring a service carried on in an orderly and dignified way. But we also may wish, sometimes, that the presence and influence of the Spirit were a little more evident in our church.

The presence and influence of the Spirit in the church described in our reading this week was certainly evident, though not in outbursts during worship. Instead, the Spirit's presence and influence is seen in the great devotion of its members and in the boldness in which the church, and especially the apostles Peter and John, proclaimed the Gospel to those around them.

We certainly desire to have that evidence of the Spirit's presence and influence among us today. That can come about as we make more fervent use of the Word as they did. May the Holy Spirit work more fervently among us as we study His Word together!

Close with the prayer in the study leaflet.

Lecture Presentation

1A   Picture of the Members of the First Congregation—Their Worship Life (2:42–43)

To pick up where we left off: The Holy Spirit, through

the foolishness of the preaching of the Word, created faith in the hearts of 3,000 people. These 3,000 were baptized and the mother of all Christian congregations was established. And now the Holy Spirit through Luke gives us some exciting and intensely interesting pictures, the first of which portrays the worship life of this congregation.

Verse 42—Continuous study of the Word, led by the apostles, resulted in a common faith, which produced an inward and outward unity called fellowship, made visible and nurtured with the celebration of the Lord's Supper and regular prayer and worship. To avoid misunderstanding what factually was happening, we need to remember that these new disciples were all Jews who were fully conversant with the Scriptures. Peter's easy use of words from David and Joel in his Pentecost sermon bear this out. The one thing Peter's hearers needed was the conviction that Jesus was the Christ. This the Holy Spirit worked in their hearts and minds on Pentecost.

Verse 43—It wasn't so much the "many wonders and miraculous signs" done by the apostles as it was this very visible witness of joy in God's Word and Sacraments made by these first converts that made such a profound impression on the rest of the city's residents.

1B Picture of the Members of the First Congregation—Their Daily Life (2:43–47)

Verses 44–45—In so large a congregation, and given the speed with which everything happened, it would only be natural that there would be those who found themselves without shelter and food. As these needs became known in these meetings, no questions were asked, no resolutions were passed, no committees were formed. Love simply acted. Verse 46—Homes were opened and meals were shared. And there was a happiness and a sincerity that was unmistakable. When actions attract, as they plainly did here, questions will be asked. Then teaching the Word takes place naturally, and the Holy Spirit can and does create faith and growth happens.

What about us? Why are many Christian congregations today not growing but declining in membership? What do the unbelievers see and hear as they watch us and the activities of our congregations? If this first congregation is to be the model of all the Christian congre-

gations to follow, then we need to do more than admire and praise them. We need to imitate them in that one quality that made them shine like lights in the night—the Spirit-given ability to openly, honestly, unhesitatingly "love one another." For you see: (1 John 3:16) "This is how we know what love is: Jesus Christ laid down His life for us. And we ought to lay down our lives for our brothers."

2 The Lord Again Reaches Thousands (3:1–10)

As He did at Pentecost, the Lord again turned to the first of His two strategies for reaching the unbelieving with His Word of pardon and peace in Christ. We call this His centripetal strategy, which simply means that He causes an event to happen that draws the unbelievers to the Word, the center of the faith. (We'll go into more detail on this when we come to Acts 8.)

Verse 1—Luke proceeds to graphically portray the event and the result. Peter and John were on their way to the temple for the daily prayer service. Verse 2—Another everyday event was taking place. Verse 3—As Peter and John were passing a well-known beggar on their way into the temple, the beggar respectfully asked them for some money.

Verses 4–10—This time the beggar received a gift beyond his wildest dreams. One of the two men said some words and reached out and took his right hand. To the beggar's absolute astonishment, he found himself being pulled off the cot. He could stand! More than that, without any physical therapy he could walk and jump as though he had done this all his life. Praising God at the top of his voice, he walked and jumped through the crowd of hundreds of people gathered for worship that afternoon, and all of them recognized him as their well-known beggar.

How perfectly the Lord set the scene for the widest possible exposure for the message of His love, forgiveness, peace, joy, and hope in Christ Jesus. That was the sole purpose of this event. And nothing has changed. The passionate desire of the Lord that all people everywhere hear about Him and His love for them in Christ clearly lies behind all of the world history that swirls about us with such an intensity and a fury today. That purpose is still the sole reason you and I are alive today and lies behind much of what happens in our lives. Holy Spirit, give us eyes to see that we may "make the most of every opportunity" (Colossians 4:5).

3 The Opportunity Seized and the Result (3:11–26; 4:4)

As the Lord intended, so it happened. Let's join the crowd and listen, for Peter's words speak also to us.

Verse 12—Peter first makes certain all the people understand that neither he nor John made this man to walk by their own power and immediately directs attention elsewhere. Verse 13—And he leaves no doubt as to the elsewhere—directing his hearers and us to the source of this healing power, "the God of Abraham, Isaac and Jacob, the God of our fathers" and "His servant Jesus." Verses 13–15—Then with startling suddenness and a directness that is crushing, Peter speaks personally to each one in the audience. This Jesus—the source of the healing that stands before you—"you handed Him over to be killed, and you disowned Him before Pilate." More than that, "you killed the author of life."

The hammer blows of the Law pounding and crushing, exposing sin and sinfulness for what they really are, were followed almost in the same breath with the most unbelievable and joyous words human ears can ever hear—the Gospel. Verse 15—With one stroke God nullified all we had done, accepting the sacrifice of His Son for all mankind and validating that great truth when He "raised Him from the dead."

Verses 16–19—Peter adds that the onlookers could all see for themselves what had happened. Accept what you see and hear, Peter urges his hearers, and repent, and your sins will be wiped out.

Peter uses the concept of erasing to describe the totality and beauty of God's forgiveness of our sins in Christ. Those of us still troubled with guilt over past sins are making ourselves miserable over something God simply cannot understand. As impossible as it is for us to make erased words on a blackboard reappear, so impossible is it for our God to remember sins that have been erased with the blood of Jesus.

Verse 4:4—The result of this clear preaching of the Law and the Gospel? Exactly what the Lord intended: "Many who heard the message believed, and the number of men grew to about five thousand." Without the Word the Holy Spirit doesn't work, but give Him the bridge of the Word to walk into people's hearts and watch out!

4 Satan Finally Makes His Move (4:1–7)

Until now, the Lord had held Satan completely in check, giving the young church time to grow in numbers and in maturity of faith. Now it was time for testing, and the Lord allowed Satan a little operating room.

There was a group ready to be used by Satan. They were called the Sadducees and were members of the Sanhedrin, the supreme Jewish court. Though small in number, they were powerful and influential because the family of the high priest and a number of other priests belonged to their group. They claimed that this life is the whole of existence and that souls die with the bodies, that there are neither angels nor spirits, and that there is no resurrection of the dead. Perfect tools for Satan, but what a sad commentary on the state of true faith among the Jewish leaders!

Verse 2—No wonder the Sadducees were greatly disturbed: Peter was preaching the very doctrine they opposed, saying the One they had caused to be nailed to a cross had risen from the dead and pointing to the healed lame man as evidence of Jesus' living power. Verse 3—Ignoring the crowd, the temple police were ordered to seize Peter and John and lock them up for the night to await trial the next morning. We can almost hear the stunned silence of the crowd and feel the shock as word of this rippled through the congregation. It must have been a long night for Peter and John.

Verse 5—But morning came and the call went out to the members of the Sanhedrin living in Jerusalem to assemble for the trial. The former and present high priests and families are mentioned by Luke since they were Sadducees and were responsible for the arrest and trial. As they assembled, Peter and John, two former fishermen from Galilee, were brought into the room and found themselves facing the most powerful judges in their nation, whose verdict had been absolutely determined in advance.

5 "One Little Word Can Fell Him!" (4:8–22)

Jesus had told the disciples, (Matthew 10:19–20) "When they arrest you, do not worry about what to say or how to say it. At that time you will be given what to say, for it will not be you speaking, but the Spirit of your Father speaking through you." One wonders if Peter and John did not use this as their devotion before sleeping soundly during the night! Luke wants us to know that there is a difference this time in Peter being filled with the Holy Spirit. This is the first of a long line of fulfillments of the promise of the Lord. There could yet come a day when we may find ourselves facing a similar situation. We need to remember that that promise is as valid for us today as when Peter and John faced their accusers.

Nothing was said about disturbing the peace or an unauthorized assembly in the temple, which might have been legitimate charges. Not even what they had done was asked about. Completely blinded by their hatred of Jesus of Nazareth, whom they regarded as a rank blasphemer because He called Himself the Son of God, and livid over all this talk about resurrection, these judges challenged the way and the means by which the healing was claimed to have been done. The end certainly did not justify the means, no matter how blessed the result, especially if the power and name of that hated "blasphemer" were involved.

The Holy Spirit's answer through Peter is clear and straight to the point and contains one of the great Gospel statements of the Scripture. Boldly implying that there was no reason for this meeting, Peter nevertheless answered their questions: Verse 10—"It is by the name of Jesus Christ of Nazareth, whom you crucified but whom God raised from the dead." Note the clashing opposites: whom you crucified, whom God raised! As undeniable and living proof of this truth, Peter pointed to the healed man who was now standing with them.

Verse 11—Before the Sadducees and Pharisees could open their mouths to respond, Peter nailed this great truth home with a quotation from their own beloved and revered David (Psalm 118:22). Verse 12—Then comes that great statement—remember who the author is!—that puts steel in our spine, boldness in our preaching, and confidence in our witnessing: "no one else"; "no other name." Jesus comes to us by means of His name (Word). That name creates faith. And by our faith in His name, He saves us. There is no second, no substitute, no alternative faith in that name alone, which is "given to men," for all people, for all time. Again,

beyond any shadow of a doubt, we are included!

"One little Word" and Satan was stopped for now. Verses 13–17—The Sadducees, who had caused the arrest, were literally left speechless by the quiet and confident boldness of Peter and John and the presence of the healed man. Repentance and acceptance of Jesus as the Christ, their Savior? No way. Their discussion was a frightening picture of the blindness of unbelief. Were it not known throughout the city, they would even deny the miracle standing outside the door.

Verse 18—Bowing only to the fear of public reaction, the court called the accused back into the room and ordered Peter and John to stop talking (the Greek word means "not to make a sound") and teaching in the name of Jesus. No exception of any kind would be allowed. Remember, this was an order from the Sanhedrin, the supreme Jewish court, who had every right to expect full and complete compliance.

Verse 19—Again, the Holy Spirit, through Peter, gave an answer that sets forth the principle that acts as a guide in similar situations for the members of Christ's church for all time: "Judge for yourselves whether it is right in God's sight to obey you rather than God." Without a moment's hesitation and despite any trace of fear, Peter and John appealed to that court to which even the Sanhedrin must bow—God's court.

It is indeed a divine command that we obey the government (Romans 13:1), but this obedience is never absolute. When the government or any human authority commands what is clearly contrary to God, Christians are bound to obey their Lord alone. One can only pray for a return of the passion, determination, and certainty so evident in the words "We cannot help speaking about what we have seen and heard" (v. 20).

6 Boldness Prayed for and Received (4:23–31)

For the Sanhedrin the whole procedure was a disaster—some probably were wishing they had never gotten involved. For Peter and John it was a sobering and faith-strengthening experience and a clear indication that the climate had changed. Their report to the other apostles produced the same result. From now on their teaching and preaching would be done in open violation of the highest legal power and authority of their nation—the

Sanhedrin. For Jews this was a heavy reality.

Verse 24—Worthy of our serious note is what now follows. Instead of launching into a tirade against the Sanhedrin and its unjust demands, as seems to be our custom so often today, the apostles automatically turned to God and laid their case before Him in prayer. Note the very positive tone of the prayer. There was no whining or complaining or asking for a removal of the threat. Instead, we find absolute confidence that their Sovereign Lord was in control and that what had happened was but the beginning of fulfillments of what the Holy Spirit spoke through David in Psalm 2, beginning with the crucifixion of Christ.

Verse 29—And now the request. Again, note how different it is from most of our requests. They did not ask for punishment of the Sanhedrin or that God would make its threats go away. They did not ask for protection against the carrying out of these threats or anything regarding their own persons. What they pleaded for was the gift of boldly speaking the Word, no matter what the Sanhedrin might do.

"Enable Your slaves (that's what the Greek word means) to speak Your word with great boldness." Peter and John had shown this boldness, but they realized now that what was needed by all of them was more than just manly courage. What was needed was the special gift of "great boldness" from God. If God would help them keep sounding forth the Word, that's all they would ask.

Verse 31—The answer to their prayer was immediate and dramatic (miraculous). "The place where they were meeting was shaken." This shaking had no natural cause but was evidence of the omnipotent presence of the Holy Spirit. We are helped in understanding this when we keep in mind the great issue involved (vv. 19–20), and which was the subject of the prayer. By this unmistakable response, the Lord put His sanction and seal upon the principle and did it for all time to come.

Verse 31b—"And they were all filled with the Holy Spirit and spoke the Word of God boldly." This was the beginning of a spiritual heroism that is a distinctive mark of Christians wherever and whenever they find themselves under persecution.

Concluding Activities

Speak a brief prayer, perhaps asking the Holy Spirit to give us greater boldness in our witnessing for Jesus. Then make any necessary announcements, share any suggestions or comments about the enrichment magazine, and distribute study leaflet 4.

The Church Meets Both Internal and External Challenges

Acts 4:32–5:42

Preparing for the Session

Central Focus

Strengthened and blessed with a wonderful unity centered in the Gospel, the church successfully meets a challenge from within raised by hypocrisy and a challenge from without raised by the threats of the Jewish leaders.

Objectives

That participants, led by the Holy Spirit, will

1. be more aware of the seriousness of the sin of hypocrisy;

2. be willing to share their own blessings in meeting the needs of other Christians;

3. show courage in witnessing boldly for Jesus.

Notes for the small-group leaders: Lesson notes and other materials you will need begin on page 59.

Session Plan

Worship

Begin the session with the hymn printed in the study leaflet and the devotion below. Hymn accompaniments are available in denominational hymnals, such as *Lutheran Worship* (refer to hymnal index). Note: Concordia Publishing House has available *Every Voice a Song*, a 9-CD set of organ accompaniments for 180 hymns and liturgy. All the initial worship hymns in the LifeLight courses are included in this resource. It's especially helpful for mission congregations and small parishes. See the list of study resources on page 7.

Devotion

"I am really impressed!" Who of us would not be pleased to hear those words said about us? We like to impress people, to have people express admiration for us.

Some will go to great efforts to impress others. They want others to admire their success in life as evidenced by a luxurious home, an expensive car, or fashionable clothing. Some try to impress others with an up-beat, confident, take-charge manner. Some try to impress others with their generosity and self-sacrifice.

Ananias and Sapphira, a couple in the first Christian congregation, evidently tried to impress others in that way. They pretended to be very sacrificial in their generosity. They pretended to be—but weren't really.

They were being hypocritical. Hypocrisy is lying not just to people but to God. Hypocrisy is pretending to God that you are better than you are. It is saying to God that you don't need His grace but that, instead, you deserve His praise. Sometimes hypocrites are so good at their lies that they fool even themselves.

But they never fool God. This couple did not fool God either. God exposed what they were doing and gave them an opportunity to repent. But they would not repent; they persisted in their lie and brought God's judgment down upon themselves.

It was a sobering lesson for the church, and it should be a sobering lesson to us as well. We do not fool the Lord with our sins. The Lord wants to forgive those sins by leading us to acknowledge them, repent of them, and receive His forgiveness for them.

Close with the prayer in the study leaflet.

Lecture Presentation

1 Picture of True Oneness in Faith and Doctrine (4:32–37)

After the second great gain in membership and after a notable victory over their opponents, Luke takes the time to show us another picture of this first congregation. And this picture is truly all the more remarkable because all the elements for disharmony and squabbling were present! Verse 32—This congregation was now made up of a vast variety of people, old and young, rich and poor, with many differences in occupations, education, and such. Yet we hear, "All the believers were one in heart and mind."

The genuineness of this inward unity became visible in the difficult area of personal possessions and money. Those who were blessed with property and money understood that they were blessed to be a blessing to those who were not so blessed. This is food for serious thought for us: We have the same Word, and the same Holy Spirit stands ready and waiting to make us, too, more ready to share our blessings with those who have need of them.

Verses 34–35—Even though the Mosaic law forbade it, there were many beggars among the Jews. Not so in this Christian congregation. As soon as a need surfaced, the means to take care of it were provided. This does not mean that the rich made themselves poor, but when the need for new funds arose, they sold off some of their property. The proceeds from the sale were given to the apostles for fair and equitable distribution.

All the while the needy were being taken care of, the apostles continued their main task, boldly preaching the Word and testifying—more clearly and fearlessly than ever—to the resurrection of Jesus Christ, the central doctrine of our faith.

2 Satan Attacks Internally (5:1–10)

Unsuccessful in his first attempt to curtail the success of the church in proclaiming the Gospel by persecution and threats, Satan tried again to slow the church down—this time from within the congregation. And, of course, he had fertile ground, for we Christians are at one and the same time saint and sinner.

Satan used Ananias and Sapphira in this attack on the church. When the sin of coveting first reared its ugly head, instead of squelching it, those two played with it and thereby allowed the sin to grow and take over and produce the sad fruit recorded here.

This event recorded in Acts is a warning to the entire New Testament church, including us today. That these verses are not in any list of Scripture to be read in Sun-

day morning worship is both strange and interesting. And we are the poorer for it. There is so much we can learn from the tragedy of this couple. When allowed to grow, sin of any kind blinds and deceives, and hypocrites are eventually born. The offering of Ananias and Sapphira was given to people and an organization. What did God have to do with what they were doing? Sound familiar?

We have the same sinful nature they did. Because that is the case, we also need to be strong in the Lord and alert always to the danger of giving in to the temptation of greed.

3 Another Period of Peace and Growth (5:11–16)

During this time of peace, the Lord dramatically increased the miracles He worked through the apostles. Here the promise of Jesus (Mark 16:17–18) of signs that would accompany the testimony of believers is dramatically fulfilled and attests to the truth of the apostles' teaching. It's indisputable proof of His resurrection.

In direct defiance of the Sanhedrin's order, the congregation met daily and openly in an area of the temple that could easily accommodate thousands at a time. For the first time we hear about people coming from the towns surrounding Jerusalem. The success was phenomenal. Luke no longer gives numbers but talks about multitudes and crowds coming to faith. It now seemed as though the entire population of Jerusalem and even the surrounding towns would soon be won for Christ.

4 The Storm Clouds Appear Again (5:17–18)

The period of peace ended abruptly. The flagrant and public violation of their edict, the daily gathering of thousands, and the undeniable miracles fanned the anger of the Sanhedrin, especially of the Sadducees, to the boiling point. The growing number of adherents of this Jesus, now even coming from outside Jerusalem, clearly spelled loss of control, and the rage and unreasonableness of jealousy spilled over into action. Satan, again, made his move externally.

Picking a time when no one or very few members of the congregation were present, the Sadducees ordered the temple police to arrest the apostles and put them in one of the common, public jails. Suddenly, and without the least warning, the leadership of the congregation was removed and jailed as criminals. Undoubtedly, the word of what had happened swept through the congregation like a wildfire. Luke leaves the reaction of the believers to our imagination. But of one thing we can be certain—after the initial shock died down, the believers were on their knees in prayer.

5 The Clouds Momentarily Disappear (5:19–26)

Throughout the Scripture God uses the angels to care for and protect the believers until the end of time (Psalm 91:11–12). The Lord also uses His angels to thwart the attacks of Satan against His children.

The angel from the Lord wakened the apostles and miraculously opened the prison doors and led them past the guards to freedom. They were not to go into hiding but were to return to the temple in the early morning and continue their public preaching and teaching. This they did, entering the temple when the gates were first opened for the early service at dawn, teaching all who came just as they had been doing the previous afternoon.

What follows now has got to be regarded as one of the more humorous accounts in the Scripture. Picture the scene. Seventy or 72 of the most respected and revered men in Judah enter the room and take their appointed seats. The high priest briefs the assembly. There's a knock on the door. Silence fills the room as the order is given to bring in the prisoners. The door opens and in step the police. Where are the prisoners? "You won't believe this, but when we got to the prison we found everything in order. The doors were locked but when we went inside the cell, it was empty—not a single prisoner was there!"

Before the members of the Sanhedrin can react, there is another knock on the door. One of the temple priests enters and reports: "The men you put in jail are standing in the temple courts teaching the people."

Once again the blindness and stubbornness of unbelief shows itself. The Sanhedrin plunged on ahead. The captain of the police decided to bring in the apostles himself. The miracle had turned the outcome around in favor of the apostles.

6 Satan's Fury Held in Check Again (5:27–39)

Verses 27–28—It is interesting to note that the high priest completely ignored the miraculous escape when the apostles stood before him. He may have had his suspicions, but he certainly did not want these witnesses talking about angels! Instead, he zeroed in on the open and flagrant violation of the Sanhedrin's edict by the apostles. So great was their hatred of Jesus that they refused to call Him by name. And now the apostles were not only accused of filling Jerusalem with their teaching, but something new was added: They "are determined to make us guilty of this man's blood."

Those callous words spoken so glibly by the people before Pilate—"Let His blood be on us and on our children!" (Matthew 27:25)—had come back to haunt them.

Verses 29–32—Peter acted as the spokesman for the rest of the apostles by common consent. His intention is clear—not to condemn, but to win them over to faith in Christ. He drew them into the sermon at the outset: God—not just any god—but "the God of our fathers." This God "raised Jesus from the dead" whom you called accursed "by hanging Him on a tree." God exalted this Jesus as "Prince and Savior" not to condemn, but to give "repentance and forgiveness of sins." We are witnesses, as is the Holy Spirit.

Peter didn't need to fill in the details. These were men learned in the Scripture, who knew all the messianic prophecies. Verse 33—The literal meaning of the Greek word Luke uses to describe their reaction is "sawn in two" or "cut to the quick." Instead of this producing repentance, as it did on Pentecost (2:37), these men were filled with a blind and uncontrollable fury. Kill the leaders and the adherents will be scattered, and the movement will die—that was their thinking.

Verses 34–39—Then the Lord intervened. It was not yet time for persecution and death; that would come soon enough. Here, to hold back their murderous hands He used one of their own, a Pharisee. And not just any Pharisee, but a noted and respected teacher, one "honored by all the people," Gamaliel. Saul (whom we know better as Paul) was a pupil of his (22:3) and may even have been present, not as a member but as an onlooker, when Gamaliel gave his speech.

And so the Lord used one of Satan's own to hold him in check. As was his right, Gamaliel had the apostles leave the room. He then cautioned and advised his colleagues to consider the possible consequences of the rash action they were contemplating. He cited two known examples of rebel leaders and what happened to their followers after the leaders were killed. Based on those historical examples, Gamaliel offered what has become known as his famous "counsel of indecision": Be careful; do not decide; wait—wait and see!

7 The First Physical Pain Produces Joy (5:40–42)

Verse 40—They all decided to take Gamaliel's way out for the time being. The apostles were summarily called back in and ordered once again "not to speak in the name of Jesus."

This time, however, the apostles were to know that the Sanhedrin meant business. A physical punishment that would serve as a reminder for many days was ordered inflicted. The punishment of public beatings was used for the breaking of ceremonial laws, heresy, and disobedience to the Sanhedrin. The apostles were ordered to bare their backs. Each of them received 39 strokes of a rod.

While the beating was going on, there is no doubt that the apostles remembered the Savior's words: "They will hand you over to the local councils and flog you in their synagogues" (Matthew 10:17). Verse 41—This produced a reaction that must have astonished the Sanhedrin. Instead of leaving like cowering whipped dogs, the apostles picked up their cloaks and left with smiles on their faces, a song in their hearts, singing praises to their God and Lord. They regarded these disgraceful welts as badges of honor, glorying in the fact that they had been "counted worthy of suffering disgrace for the Name."

Verse 42—A new strength, courage, and boldness filled them. Never for a moment did the apostles stop their teaching and preaching. The way Luke piles up words about the apostles' activity in this postbeating period tells us that something new had been added to their lives—a sense of urgency. The days of peace appear to be growing shorter. In every place, at any time, with anyone who cared to listen, they shared the "good news that Jesus is the Christ."

As we put ourselves in these pictures Luke paints of the first congregation in Jerusalem and the activities surrounding it, we cannot help but feel chagrined and ashamed. There are no laws in our land forbidding us to talk about the faith that lives within us. No one is going to put us in jail or beat us if we share our faith in Christ with our neighbor. Why are we so often so reluctant to do so? How many of us even know if the people we work with or the neighbors who live next door know and love the Lord Jesus? Our country has been uniquely blessed with freedom and peace. But membership in the Christian churches is, for the most part, on the decline. And this at a time when the Lord has turned our country into one of the most fertile mission fields in the world! Here we have food for serious thought and prayer!

The answer doesn't lie in forming new committees or writing new and different evangelism programs. It is much simpler: the return of every member of our congregations to a structured study of the Scripture. There we will find Jesus, the source of power and strength, in that He has defeated the devil (overcome sin) for us. He sends His Spirit, who through the Word can make us "one in heart and mind" (4:32), give new meaning and purpose to our lives, and fill us with the necessary sense of urgency. Imagine what the Holy Spirit would (not could!) work in us and through us, if our Bible class attendance matched our church membership!

Concluding Activities

Speak a brief prayer, perhaps for an increased study of Scripture in the congregation(s) represented by your LifeLight assembly. Then make any necessary announcements and distribute study leaflet 5.

The Church Has Its First Martyr

Acts 6–7

Preparing for the Session

Central Focus

To allow the apostles to concentrate on their spiritual duties, the church selects seven helpers or deacons. One of them, Stephen, becomes the first Christian to give the ultimate witness to his faith—by dying because of it.

Objectives

That participants, led by the Holy Spirit, will

1. understand a God-pleasing manner of resolving disputes with fellow Christians;

2. realize that a consistent witness to Jesus may draw the opposition of unbelievers;

3. be confident of God's guidance and sustaining presence when our witness meets with hostility;

4. be courageous and have trust in God in witnessing to Jesus.

Notes for the small-group leaders: Lesson notes and other materials you will need begin on page 62.

Session Plan

Worship

Begin the session with the hymn printed in the study leaflet and the devotion below. Hymn accompaniments are available in denominational hymnals, such as *Lutheran Worship* (refer to hymnal index). Note: Concordia Publishing House has available *Every Voice a Song,* a 9-CD set of organ accompaniments for 180 hymns and liturgy. All the initial worship hymns in the LifeLight courses are included in this resource. It's especially helpful for mission congregations and small parishes. See the list of study resources on page 7.

Devotion

A chicken and a pig were thinking about surprising Farmer Brown with a special breakfast on his birthday. The chicken suggested ham and eggs. "Oh, fine!" exclaimed the pig. "For you that's a contribution; for me it's a sacrifice!"

Making a witness to Jesus also can come under those two categories. Most often speaking up for Jesus is in the contribution category; it costs us some effort, perhaps some degree of discomfort (perhaps not even that), but no more than that. But there are other times when making a witness to Jesus involves a sacrifice; it costs us something significant. It can even mean making the ultimate sacrifice—life itself. Making that ultimate sacrifice obviously calls for a lot of faith in and love for the Lord.

But countless people have made that sacrifice, through all of Christian history—including some in our own time. Some of these sacrifices—we call them martyrdoms—are known to many others. Some of these sacrifices were known to only a few and have since been forgotten. But all are known to Jesus, who welcomes these courageous witnesses to heaven with special honor. John gives us this picture from heaven: "When He [the Lamb] opened the fifth seal, I saw under the altar the souls of those who had been slain because of the word of God and the testimony they had maintained. They called out in a loud voice, 'How long, Sovereign Lord, holy and true, until You judge the inhabitants of the earth and avenge our blood?' Then each of them was given a white robe, and they were told to wait a little longer, until the number of their fellow servants and brothers who were to be killed as they had been was completed" (Revelation 6:9–11).

It is probably unlikely that we ourselves will be called upon to make that ultimate witness. But we may be certain that the Holy Spirit will sustain and be with us whenever we give our witness to Jesus, whether of the contribution or sacrifice kind!

Close with the prayer in the study leaflet.

Lecture Presentation

1 Introduction

In this lesson we are introduced to the word *martyr*—someone put to death for standing by his or her beliefs, especially belief in Jesus Christ.

Stephen is the first martyr of the Christian church. He was followed by a long line of martyrs right on up to the present day. Statisticians tell us that the number of known Christian martyrs grew from 35,600 in 1900 to 325,800 in 1989. By the year 2000 it reached 500,000. We need to understand that, of all the furies of Satan, martyrdom always backfires. The Lord allows martyrdom for His own purposes and to His glory. Those who are martyred aren't losers but victors, for they die in the Lord and are with Him forever!

2 Selection of the First Deacons (6:1–7)

How much time intervened between the persecution recorded in chapter 5 and the events we find in chapter 6 Luke does not say. Unhindered in any way, the apostles continued boldly and fearlessly teaching and preaching, and the Holy Spirit continued to bless them greatly. Verse 1—The number of disciples "was increasing" (*multiplied* is the actual word used by Luke). Given the number of times such an increase in believers has been referred to since Pentecost, very likely the congregation by now numbered somewhere between 20 and 25 thousand.

Here for the first time Luke uses the beautiful word *disciple* when writing about the increase in believers. *Disciple* means "someone who is actively following Jesus in daily life."

Twenty-five thousand members and 12 pastors! Not many congregations since then can boast of so large an active, united membership.

The large size of the congregation, which included people in so many different conditions in life, caused a minor ripple of complaint. Certain widows were being overlooked in the daily distribution of food.

Verse 2—As the leaders of the congregation, the apostles acted promptly to prevent the case from becoming

acute. Luke simply reports, "So the Twelve gathered all the disciples together." From the very outset when it came to administration and organizational details, the apostles put these matters in the hands of the congregation.

The apostles are quick to point out where their primary responsibilities lay; the obligation of the Christian ministry is "the ministry of the word of God." Administrative and operational tasks are to be turned over to others.

Verse 3—"Choose seven men from among you." Note on what basis these men were to be chosen by the congregation. There was no call for volunteers. Rather, men were chosen who were known to have received from the Holy Spirit the special gift of wisdom.

Verse 5—The entire congregation thought this was a marvelous suggestion. Luke names the seven, placing the two names that will play prominent roles in the near future at the head of the list, Stephen and Philip. These two had received additional gifts from the Holy Spirit so that they would also become the first evangelists of the church. About the remaining five nothing more is recorded.

Verse 6—The elected seven were brought before the apostles for the official transference of the administrative responsibilities.

Verse 7—And so with the ripple quieted, the apostles devoted themselves fully to the teaching and preaching of the Word of God. The Holy Spirit swept through the hearts of the hearers, and, again, the "number of disciples in Jerusalem increased rapidly." No longer are we able to even guess the total, nor is it necessary. Almost in passing—but what a victory for the Holy Spirit!—Luke reports that "a large number of priests" became believers. How distressing this must have been to the high priest and to his cohorts!

Clearly, the church is not a human institution, and its growth does not depend on committees and methods. The church, as Paul describes it, is divine; it is Christ's body here on earth. As such, Christ lives in each believer. An important contribution to that early rapid and large growth was the fact that the unbelievers could clearly see Christ in the lives of His followers. Those lives validated the teachings of the apostles.

Food for thought: Could it just be possible that one of

the reasons for the rapid growth of the Muslim religion and the continued gradual decline of the adherents to Christ is that their lives validate what they teach and ours don't?

3 Days of Peace Draw to a Close (6:8–14)

Verse 8—Luke draws special attention to the additional special gifts the Lord gave to Stephen. "Full of God's grace and power" refers to the special favor of God that conferred on him the power to perform miracles when and where the Lord desired. The congregation had made him a deacon, and we can be sure he carried out those responsibilities faithfully. But the Lord also graciously singled out Stephen as His instrument through whom He worked miracles. His purpose in doing this would very soon become clear.

Verses 9–10—The wonders and miracles the Lord performed through Stephen drew attention to him. A fairly large group of men confronted Stephen probably multiple times on the street. Luke writes simply, "They could not stand up against his wisdom or the Spirit by whom he spoke."

Verse 11—Frustrated and angry, these men's minds become fertile ground for the father of lies, Satan. Determined to stop Stephen and bring him to trial, they stooped to the same tactic the Sanhedrin used at the trial of Jesus—false witnesses. These liars said they had heard Stephen speak "against Moses and against God"—words sure to brand Stephen as the worst of blasphemers.

Verse 12—With this Satanic plot in hand, Stephen's enemies went to work spreading this lie in the right places. Stephen was brought before the Sanhedrin for trial.

Verses 13–14—The same type of quotation that was used by the false witnesses at the trial of Jesus (Mark 14:56–59) was used here.

4 Stephen's Bold and Pointed Defense (6:15–7:56)

Verse 15—But before the trial could begin, something startling happened: "They saw that his face was like the face of an angel." We recall again the promise of Jesus given to the disciples that at their trials the Holy Spirit would inspire them and speak through them.

The Sanhedrin members were struck by the phenomenon—struck but not moved. In spite of themselves, a hush fell on the room, and they were gripped by that light on Stephen's face until his answer to them reached its climax. How could Luke possibly have known this? There were witnesses enough, and one especially was a young Pharisee named Saul, later to become Paul, the greatest missionary of the Gospel and Luke's dearest friend.

Verse 7:1—To give at least the appearance of a trial, the high priest asked Stephen if the charges of blasphemy were true. Filled with the Holy Spirit, as his face indicated, Stephen began in a quiet tone and proceeded with studied deliberation.

Verses 2–50—Throughout his address Stephen wove the record of the disobedience and unbelief of the people of Israel and their leaders. Joseph was sold by his wicked brothers (v. 9). Moses was scorned (vv. 25–28)—the very Moses whom God made a deliverer (v. 35), the very Moses who spoke the great Messianic promise about the Prophet like himself (v. 37), the very Moses whom the whole nation refused to obey (vv. 39–43).

Verses 51–53—Though he started very calmly, Stephen concluded powerfully. Using the tone and manner of the old prophets, he gave a stinging denunciation of Israel's stubborn unbelief, intended to bring repentance and healing. He repeated the same charge of killing the prophets that Jesus made (Matthew 23:37; Luke 13:34) and drove it home: "And now you!" The very ones to whom the Law had been given stood convicted of utterly breaking and abandoning the Law.

Verse 54—The tables were completely turned. Stephen had put his accusers, the witnesses, and the court itself on the defensive. They became utterly hostile. The hearts of Stephen's hearers did not bend in contrition. The outward evidence that this had happened was that they began grinding their teeth at him in suppressed rage.

Verse 55—It was then that something wonderful happened for Stephen. He became filled with the Holy Spirit in a special way and as he looked up toward heaven he "saw the glory of God, and Jesus standing at the right hand of God."

The first martyr of the Christian faith was going to his death. He is the first of a long, long line of future martyrs. This special sight was given to him not as though it were intended for him and his strengthening alone, but through him for all who were to follow. The glory of God shines for all of them as they near death. The Savior stands ready to receive them. Through Stephen's eyes they are all to see and rejoice.

And so the Holy Spirit Himself completed Stephen's address for him in a most miraculous way with the most powerful Gospel word. Unlike Peter, Stephen did not need to preach the resurrection of Christ. Here Jesus Himself preached it by revealing Himself to Stephen in His heavenly glory and causing Stephen to tell the Sanhedrin what his eyes were seeing.

It had to be obvious that Stephen was telling them what his eyes were seeing right at that moment—Jesus, whom they crucified, was standing in the heavens as the eternal King at God's own right hand of majesty and power.

Whom were they opposing? The glorified Son of Man and the heavenly, eternal almighty Son of God!

5 Satan's Fury Allowed Full Reign (7:57–58)

Stephen's witness, although preached through a miracle of the Holy Spirit, snapped the control of the Sanhedrin. Yelling at the top of their lungs and covering their ears so they would not hear any more of this "blasphemy," all legal formalities were thrown to the winds as mob violence suddenly took over. Immediately Stephen was surrounded. His long, loose outer robes were stripped off and were thrown at the feet of a young man named Saul. Stones were picked up and thrown at Stephen in blind rage and hate.

6 But "The Kingdom Ours Remaineth!" (7:59–60)

Verse 59—Stone after stone struck Stephen, breaking bones and producing deep cuts. He raised his face to his Savior and prayed after the pattern of Jesus' own dying prayer: "Lord Jesus, receive my spirit." Instantly heard, Stephen's spirit was received by Jesus into the glory and bliss of heaven.

Verse 60—Driven to his knees by the blows from the stones, at the very moment of his death, Stephen made one last attempt to reach his enemies and the crowd. At the top of his voice, so that all in the crowd heard, Stephen prayed his final prayer: "Lord, do not hold this

sin against them." This prayer for his enemies he had learned from his Savior (Luke 23:34).

Then "he fell asleep." This is the beautiful way the Scripture describes the death of the believer—and only the believer. Violent and terrible as was his form of death, Stephen nevertheless literally "fell asleep." So do all believers. By use of this phrase for death, our belief in the resurrection of the body at the last day is affirmed. Stephen's soul now lives with His Savior, awaiting the reunion with his body on the Last Day: "Where, O death, is your victory? Where, O death, is your sting? . . . But thanks be to God! He gives us the victory through our Lord Jesus Christ" (1 Corinthians 15:55–57).

Concluding Activities

Speak a brief prayer, perhaps thanking God for the courageous witness of all who, like Stephen, have been murdered for the sake of the Gospel. Then make any necessary announcements and distribute study leaflet 6.

The Church Takes the Gospel to Samaria and Beyond

Acts 8

Preparing for the Session

Central Focus

Persecution causes Christians to be scattered from Jerusalem into remote areas of Judea and into Samaria (as Christ had said). In those places they courageously and effectively proclaimed the Gospel to Jews, Samaritans, and—in one case—to a visitor from Ethiopia.

Objectives

That participants, led by the Holy Spirit, will

1. be aware of Christ's two mission strategies: bringing people to the Word and bringing the Word to people;

2. recognize that what appears to us to be a setback can actually be meant as a special opportunity to witness for Christ;

3. be alert for special opportunities to share the Gospel with others;

4. be ready to share the Gospel with people without regard to their racial, ethnic, economic, or social background.

Notes for the small-group leaders: Lesson notes and other materials you will need begin on page 65.

Session Plan

Worship

Begin the session with the hymn printed in the study leaflet and the devotion below. Hymn accompaniments are available in denominational hymnals, such as *Lutheran Worship* (refer to hymnal index). Note: Concordia Publishing House has available *Every Voice a Song*, a 9-CD set of organ accompaniments for 180 hymns and liturgy. All the initial worship hymns in the LifeLight courses are included in this resource. It's especially helpful for mission congregations and small parishes. See the list of study resources on page 7.

Devotion

Perhaps you are familiar with the "that's bad—no, that's good" jokes. Chapter 8 of Acts might seem to lend itself to that sort of story.

> "Persecution broke out against Christians in Jerusalem."
>
> "That's bad."
>
> "No, that's good. It caused the Christians to take the Gospel to Samaria."

God can—and does—use what at first looks like a setback to achieve something great. It happened then, and it can happen now.

I don't know about you, but I often suffer setbacks. But I also often see how the Lord uses those setbacks to bring about something good in my life. He sometimes uses them to give me an opportunity to share the Gospel in an unexpected way.

Close with the prayer in the study leaflet.

Lecture Presentation

1 Introduction

By now we've caught some pretty plain glimpses of the Lord at work for and on behalf of His church. We are going to see a lot more. What we need to grasp fully is that not just some things, but everything that happens throughout the world is in some way—whether we can understand it or not—related to the Lord's intense desire that everyone hear about His love for them in Christ. Listen carefully as Christ succinctly tells us why the end hasn't come. "And this gospel of the kingdom will be preached in the whole world as a testimony to all nations, and *then* the end will come" (Matthew 24:14).

In all of this the Lord uses only two strategies. Being able to recognize these and understand them completes the operation on our eyes, and we will see more clearly the single purpose and meaning behind all that the Lord is doing in our world. And the two strategies? Through events and happenings of all kinds—political oppressions, economic and natural disasters—the Lord is either *bringing people to the Word* or *carrying the Word to people*. Apply either of these strategies to a world happening and we get a new and exciting understanding of God at work in this world.

One of the two strategies, carrying the Word to the people, is the one we almost exclusively associate with missions—going into all the world by sending missionaries. But the second strategy, where the Lord brings the people to the Gospel, is a strategy that the Lord also is using mightily in our world today.

Throughout the Scripture, beginning with Noah, and again in the chapter before us, we see the Lord setting the stage, moving the furniture, and opening the doors. One action the Lord will not take: He Himself will not talk to this world directly; that, He says, is why He left us here, why we live where we live, work where we work, play where we play. What an awesome responsibility, but what an exciting reason for living! Today, O Lord, may "the lives that my life touches, However great or small—let them through me see Jesus, Who served and saved us all" (from the hymn "On Galilee's High Mountain," by Henry L. Lettermann, © 1982 CPH).

2 "And in All Judea and Samaria" (8:1–3)

As we know, the congregation in Jerusalem had grown to be extremely large. The Holy Spirit kept blessing the teaching and preaching, and new members were multiplied daily from the city and the surrounding towns. How easy to forget that the Savior had said something about going out to Judea and Samaria and the rest of the world. After all, the matter of the needy had been settled peaceably. They were once again of one heart and mind, studying the Word and waiting for Christ's return. Wasn't that what He said they were to do?

But it was now the Lord's time to move His children out. And so He allowed the blessing of persecution. For only a short time Satan would use Saul as the prime mover in this persecution. While Saul may not have thrown a stone, he nevertheless thoroughly agreed with Stephen's death.

Since he agreed with what had just happened, the next obvious step was to crush the entire Christian movement. And he wasted no time attempting to do just that. A house-to-house search by a force of police under Saul's command and with the full blessing of the Sanhedrin began. Where Christians—men and women—were found, they were rudely dragged from their homes and summarily thrown into prison, facing possible execution without a hearing or trial.

And the result of this great persecution? Exactly what Jesus ordered. "When you are persecuted in one place, flee to another" (Matthew 10:23). A mass exodus from Jerusalem of all the Christians not imprisoned rapidly took place—that is, by all except the apostles. Luke gives no reason; he just states the fact. Evidently, the Lord wanted Jerusalem to remain the headquarters for work among the Jews until He would direct them elsewhere.

3 And the Word Grows in Samaria (8:4–13)

How far these scattered Christians went Luke tells us in chapter 11: "as far as Phoenicia, Cyprus and Antioch" (v. 19). And wherever they went, they talked about why they had to leave Jerusalem and about their faith in the Lord Jesus Christ.

It is extremely important to note well that Christian churches were first planted in all these places through the talking, teaching, and yes, even preaching of lay people deeply in love with their Savior. Remember how persecution always backfires? Saul thought he was crushing the Christian movement. In reality, the harder he worked to stop Christianity, the more he himself helped to spread it.

Verses 5–8—For now Luke concentrates on the growth of the church in Samaria. One of the seven deacons, Philip, ended up there, probably in the city of Shechem at the foot of Mount Gerizim, the center of Samaritan worship.

Philip preached boldly throughout the city. The Holy Spirit gave him the gift to perform miracles of healing and the power to drive out demons. These special signs God gave to certain Christians for a time to attest to the resurrection of Christ and His complete victory over the powers of Satan and hell.

Verses 9–13—Among the people who heard Philip's words and witnessed his miracles and power was a man named Simon. Before Philip came to the city, Simon was one of the most powerful persons in all of Samaria. He had most of the people under his control with astonishing feats of magic and the satanic practice of black arts.

Luke here paints a powerful picture of contrast. Simon's hold on the people was not only powerful and deep, but of long duration. Philip was the new kid on the block, and overnight Simon's hold on the people was shattered. The people were flocking to Philip, confessing their faith in Christ, and being baptized. Simon decided to listen to Philip and, to his astonishment and joy, found himself believing and asking to be baptized.

The miracles and signs done through Philip astonished the people and got their attention initially. But it was the Gospel that Philip preached that brought about the change and worked faith. Luke makes that very clear. Philip preached "the good news of the kingdom of God and the name of Jesus Christ" (v. 12), and hearts and lives were changed as the Holy Spirit used that all-powerful Gospel Word to create faith.

4 The Church Is One and Is for All (8:14–17)

Word of the Spirit's success through Philip in Samaria reached the apostles in Jerusalem. One can almost feel the joy and excitement! What appeared to have been a major setback the Lord turned into a rich blessing with an unbelievable harvest—and in Samaria—of all places, Samaria!

At this point it is important to refresh our memories about Samaria and the Samaritans. This will help us better understand what follows. Samaria was located between Galilee on the north and Judea on the south. The Jews regarded the Samaritans as socially and religiously inferior, so much so that if their business took them from Judea to Galilee, they took the road around Samaria. No self-respecting Jew would walk on Samaritan land or talk to a Samaritan (see John 4:9). Here we have a racial prejudice like the one that, all too sadly, continues to rear its ugly head in our country today.

Verses 15–16—Should there be two separate but equal churches or just one? The Holy Spirit answered that question conclusively when Peter and John arrived for their visit to Philip and the new congregation. Why else would Peter and John pray that these new believers "might receive the Holy Spirit"? Had not the Holy Spirit through Word and Sacrament brought them to faith, and was He not already living in their hearts?

Verse 17—And now the question. Would these Samaritan believers receive the same outward signs of the Spirit's inner presence, thereby assuring them they were true members in the body of Christ? Luke's brevity is sometimes frustrating. He simply states, "Then Peter and John" after prayer "placed their hands on them, and they received the Holy Spirit." And it happened! The Holy Spirit miraculously distributed His charismatic gifts to those Samaritan believers on whose heads the apostles laid their hands. They, too, could speak in tongues and perform miracles of healing (1 Corinthians 12:7–13). No doubt they were filled with excitement and joy—not so much because of the miraculous powers they suddenly had, but because this was indisputable proof that they were one with all believers in Christ!

5 Another Important Example (8:18–25)

Verses 18–19—"All these [gifts] are the work of one and the same Spirit, and He gives them to each one, just as He determines" (1 Corinthians 12:11). Such is the lesson we are to learn from what Luke now records. Simon, whom we spoke of earlier, saw what happened when Peter and John laid their hands on some of the people. He remembered his old control and power over the people, and the sins of envy and jealousy reared their ugly head in his heart. If only he could do the same thing that Peter and John did. Simon had paid out money to learn his old tricks, and so he now offers money to Peter and John if they would teach him how to perform these new and astonishing feats.

Here we have the second glaring example of the destructive belief, sadly still used by Satan today, that money can buy what can only be obtained by and from the grace of God. Verses 20–21—As it should have been, Peter's rebuke was severe. By such a request Simon had excluded himself from ever receiving any of the gifts themselves.

Verses 22–23—Peter urged Simon to have a genuine change of heart concerning his attitude and to turn to the Lord for forgiveness. Verse 24—The Holy Spirit worked the change in Simon's heart, and he tasted the full joy and peace of Christ's forgiveness. And there was joy among the angels in heaven!

6 The Lord Opens the Door to Africa (8:26–40)

Verse 26—Now we go back to Philip. Philip had just had another day of continued preaching and teaching of the Word with phenomenal success. He dropped off into a peaceful and happy sleep, eager to continue in the morning. But the Lord had other things in mind for Philip. An angel suddenly appeared to Philip and told him that the Lord needed him somewhere else.

Verse 27—With clear instructions as to where he was to go—back through Jerusalem and on to the desert road between Jerusalem and Gaza—Philip set out. Long before Philip met the eunuch from Ethiopia the Lord had been setting the stage. He had chosen to bring the Gospel to Africa not through one of the apostles but through one of Ethiopia's own citizens, a person of great political importance. Though not named here, he was the royal treasurer for the Ethiopian queen.

We might imagine what had preceded this event. Perhaps this man had been sent often by his queen to Jerusalem on business (the Lord bringing the unbeliever to the Word), and on one of these trips this official came to accept the Jewish faith. This time it seems that he made the 200-mile trip on his own to worship his newfound God.

Verse 28—While in Jerusalem, he evidently did something unprecedented—he bought a scroll of Scripture. Remember, there were no bookstores with scrolls just lying around for purchase. The purchase of this scroll must have cost him a pretty penny! But, more important, note the hand of God at work, for it was surely the Lord's providence that had placed Isaiah, the evangelist of the Old Testament, into this searching man's hands and caused him to be reading the choicest part of the book when Philip caught up to him.

Verse 29—The Spirit directed Philip to the chariot on the dusty desert road. We can't help wondering what Philip thought he would find. Verse 30—Imagine Philip's astonishment as he came alongside the chariot and heard the man reading aloud from the prophet Isaiah!

The Lord had brought the Ethiopian man to where he might hear the Word. Now the second strategy of the Lord, bringing the Word to the unbeliever, moved into action. Verses 31–35—Philip joined the man in his chariot, answered his questions, and told him about Jesus. As Philip was talking, the Holy Spirit opened the man's eyes and created faith in his heart in Jesus Christ. The result? Verse 36–38—His faith was sealed in Baptism. And he became the Lord's instrument in bringing the message of salvation in the name of Jesus to his homeland, beginning with his queen.

Verse 39–40—Luke says nothing more about this man, but we need know nothing more. The Lord used this one man to bring His Gospel to Ethiopia and from there into all of northern Africa.

Back to Philip. In one instant he was baptizing the Ethiopian, and in the next he found himself many miles away in Azotus. We are told only that Philip continued to preach in the coastal towns, finally stopping at Caesarea, where he apparently made his home.

Concluding Activities

Conclude with a brief prayer, perhaps that the Lord might use all of us to witness more effectively for Him where He has put us. Then make any necessary announcements and distribute study leaflet 7.

The Church Receives an Unlikely Convert

Acts 9:1–31

Preparing for the Session

Central Focus

A dramatic conversion occurs when Saul, on his way to Damascus to arrest Christians and bring them to Jerusalem for punishment, is stopped and overcome by Jesus. Saul repents, is baptized, and is transformed from a persecutor to a preacher of the faith he had come to destroy.

Objectives

That participants, led by the Holy Spirit, will

1. recognize the grace of God in Saul's conversion and enlistment as a missionary;

2. be grateful for God's grace in their own coming to faith in Jesus and in being given a part in His kingdom;

3. more readily forgive and accept those who have sinned against them;

4. rely more consistently on God's grace in their own daily lives.

Notes for the small-group leaders: Lesson notes and other materials you will need begin on page 67.

Session Plan

Worship

Begin the session with the hymn printed in the study leaflet and the devotion below. Hymn accompaniments are available in denominational hymnals, such as *Lutheran Worship* (refer to hymnal index). Note: Concordia Publishing House has available *Every Voice a Song*, a 9-CD set of organ accompaniments for 180 hymns and liturgy. All the initial worship hymns in the

LifeLight courses are included in this resource. It's especially helpful for mission congregations and small parishes. See the list of study resources on page 7.

Devotion

A woman rounded a curve on a country highway on a snowy winter Sunday morning, suddenly encountered a patch of ice, and skidded off the highway into an adjoining cemetery. She got out of her car, noticed the church on the other side of the cemetery, and walked over to announce to the startled parishioners on their way into worship, "I have concluded that the Lord wants me to worship here this morning."

Have you ever been stopped in your tracks and concluded that it was the Lord's doing? That certainly was the case with Saul in our Bible study for this week. Perhaps it also has been the case with you.

Oh, you may not have seen the risen Christ in a vision as Saul did. But you may have been convinced, anyway, that the Lord had suddenly grabbed you and said, "Whoa!" It may have been a time when you suddenly found yourself flat on your back on a hospital bed. Or when your life took a jolting turn. Or when you were given the abrupt realization that your life was going in absolutely the wrong direction.

Sometimes the Lord, in His grace, does reach out and grab us, as He did Saul. In His mercy He takes hold of us and gives our lives a new turn. We may be surprised by the suddenness (or even the roughness) of His action, but afterwards we realize how gracious the Lord has been. Paul could not stop praising the grace of God that had literally knocked him down on the Damascus road. Neither will we!

Close with the prayer in the study leaflet.

Lecture Presentation

1 Satan's Fury Reaches a Feverish Pitch (9:1–2)

Verses 1–2—Luke's description of Saul's fanatic zeal reminds us of Peter's description of Satan: "Your enemy the devil prowls around like a roaring lion looking for someone to devour" (1 Peter 5:8). Many believers followed Stephen to martyrdom without a trial or sentence. Luke rightly calls this action of Saul "murder." It is clear that the apostles were still needed, for they remained under the protecting hand of the Lord in Jerusalem. Saul went to the high priest for the necessary letters of authority to arrest men and women "who belonged to the Way." "I am the way," Jesus had said (John 14:6). So the persecution was really against Christ, as Saul would soon learn.

Saul chose to go to Damascus, the oldest continuously inhabited city in the world, already a city in Abraham's day (Genesis 14:15; 15:2). Why Damascus, a city almost 140 miles away, and not Samaria? There are three logical reasons. The Sanhedrin had no jurisdiction in Samaria. The Roman emperors had granted the Sanhedrin authority over Jews living outside of Palestine, and a large number of Jews were living and working in Damascus and had built a number of synagogues. Saul apparently assumed, or had gotten word, that a fair number of the followers of "the Way" who fled his violent activities in Jerusalem had gotten as far as Damascus, had settled there, and were spreading (what he viewed as) their false teachings. This had to be nipped in the bud.

2 The Lord Dramatically Intervenes (9:3–9)

What now follows is Luke's historical account. Saul (who would later be called Paul) embellishes this account with additional details in two of his speeches (Acts 22:3–16 and 26:12–18) and in three of his letters (1 Corinthians 9:1 and 15:8; Galatians 1:11–24; 1 Timothy 1:12–13). A reading of these personal accounts will help us to fill in some details that Luke omits without our having to make constant reference to where we got such information.

To summarize verses 3–9: A flash of extreme light knocks Saul from his horse. All see the light; only Saul hears the voice of Jesus. Now blind, Saul is led to Damascus, where he begins a three-day fast. His fearful sins lay heavily upon him. Shut off from the world, blind, abstaining from food, with no one to help him, his proud pharisaical self-righteousness was crushed and conquered. There remained only a sinner in the dust of

hopeless contrition. Sometimes the Lord must crush our proud hearts too so we might be prepared to accept His forgiveness.

3 "This Man Is My Chosen Instrument!" (9:10–19)

Verses 10–12—The Lord now went to another home in Damascus where a disciple named Ananias lived. The Lord came to Ananias in a vision. Verse 13—It is not hard to imagine the absolute astonishment that must have run through Ananias at the Lord's message. With simple openness he said, in effect: "Hey, wait a minute, Lord! Let me tell You what others have told me about this Saul. We all know why he has come to Damascus."

By the way, notice that here we have the first use of the word *saints* in referring to believers. This came to be a standard term for believers in the New Testament. Saints are those who have experienced and still experience the forgiving and sanctifying undeserved favor (grace) of God.

Verse 15–16—And Christ answered Ananias, in effect: "Just get going; everything is all right! This man is My chosen instrument!" What a God! What a Lord! What a Savior! If anyone studying this feels they have sinned so deeply and shamefully they can't be forgiven, take heart and drink deeply! Everything about Saul's life, including where he was born, his natural Roman citizenship, his secular and religious training, yes, even the fact that he had been a persecutor of the One he would now serve for the rest of his life—everything had been preparing for this moment. Through all this the Lord had chosen Saul to be the one who would "carry My name before the Gentiles and their kings."

Verse 17—What a beautiful and strong faith we see in Ananias! He went to the house and found Saul waiting for him just as the Lord had said. No hesitation, no revulsion.

One could only wish that Ananias's forgiveness and acceptance of his former enemy were more visible in the church today. What was key to Ananias's genuine and total acceptance of this despicable excuse of a human being? On his way over to Saul's he remembered that in God's eyes he also was a despicable excuse of a human being, and that Christ, without any conditions, had forgiven and accepted him. Could he do any less with Saul?

We who bear the title of "saints" should remember that no other person can do to us in a lifetime what we do to and against our Lord each day. And He richly and daily and unconditionally forgives us and cleanses us from all sins with His holy and precious blood. Can we do any less?

4 From Persecutor to Apostle and Preacher (9:20–22)

Saul had seen Christ. He now preached as an eyewitness. Remember also that he had been a brilliant student of Gamaliel and was competent, therefore, to teach the Scriptures. This gave him access to the synagogues. The more Saul preached, the more power the Holy Spirit gave him, and the more he baffled and stymied the Jews, proving that Jesus is the Christ.

5 A Taste of His Own Medicine! (9:23–25)

Verse 12—The "many days" of Saul's stay in Damascus amounted to about three years (Galatians 1:18). During part of those years Saul visited Arabia. We know the fact of this visit but nothing about the specific place, the duration, or the purpose. It certainly wasn't for the purpose of preaching and establishing churches, or Luke would surely have written about it. All we can surmise is that the two periods when Paul disappeared—his brief jaunt into Arabia and his eight-year stay in or near his home of Tarsus—were periods used by the Lord to train and hone the apostle for his great missionary journeys into the world of the Gentiles.

Saul returned to Damascus and renewed his vigorous activity of preaching and teaching. But then the climate changed dramatically. The Jews who wouldn't be convinced called a meeting and passed a resolution to have Saul killed. Verse 24—Saul learned about the plot in some way and went into hiding. Since the gates of the walled city were sealed, Saul's enemies were confident it would only be a matter of time until Saul was found and murdered. They watched and watched and watched. And all the while Saul was already on his way to Jerusalem.

Verse 25—Saul's escape was really very simple. Some of the houses that adjoined the wall around the city had

windows that were high above the wall itself. From such a window, strong and loving hands lowered Saul to the ground in a basket.

6 Back at the Capital (9:26–30)

Verse 26—Saul had been gone for almost three years. During that time the political scene had changed. War had broken out between Herod and King Aretas, so that there had been little or no communication between Damascus and Jerusalem for a while. Suddenly Saul, the persecutor, reappeared out of nowhere. Nobody believed that he was actually a disciple of the Lord Christ as he now claimed to be. It seemed incredible that this most violent persecutor of the Christians, who had caused so many to flee their homes and businesses and had caused so much heartache and pain, was himself now a Christian.

Verse 27—Finally, Barnabas came to Saul's rescue. Barnabas took Saul to the one Saul had been waiting to meet—Peter. James, the head elder of the Jerusalem congregation, was also present. (From Galatians 1:19 we learn that other apostles were busy elsewhere). Barnabas very pointedly conveyed to Peter and James—and through them to the rest of the apostles—that Saul was not merely another believer, but that, beyond any shadow of a doubt, the Lord had qualified and made him a fellow apostle. Saul had the essential qualification for the title of apostle—he had seen the risen and glorified Christ.

Verses 28–29—It appears that whenever Saul bumped into a Grecian Jew as he walked the streets in Jerusalem during his brief stay, he engaged this person in conversation and finally debate that Jesus is the Christ. Their reaction? They plotted to kill him.

One morning Saul went to the temple for prayer. While praying, Christ again appeared visibly to him and ordered him: "Leave Jerusalem immediately, because they will not accept your testimony about Me" (Acts 22:18). Saul answered his Lord with a very logical argument. He wanted to stay in Jerusalem because he felt his witness for the Lord here would be very powerful.

Christ's answer to Saul was simple and direct. It was also a commissioning, reaffirming the words Ananias had spoken to him in Judas's home: "Go; I will send you far away to the Gentiles" (22:21).

Verse 30—Saul told Peter and James what the Lord had just told him. A small but trusted delegation got Saul safely to the seaport town of Caesarea and then on a ship for his hometown of Tarsus. Luke tells us nothing about why Saul went home to Tarsus, nor what he did during the eight years he stayed there. There Saul remained until Barnabas came to Tarsus to bring Saul back into the picture.

7 Time of Peace and Growth Again (9:31)

"Then the church throughout Judea, Galilee and Samaria enjoyed a time of peace." This is the first time Luke mentions Galilee, but in so doing he is telling us that the church was well established throughout these three provinces. With the use of the Greek word *ecclesia* for church, Luke is stating that there were not three churches, but one church united in faith and doctrine and life.

Luke points us again to the source of power and growth for the Lord's church. Not committees, programs, projects, or human plans, but immersion in the Word through which the Holy Spirit strengthens and matures our faith, so that the disciples' lives were living reflections of Christ for all the world to see. Lord, fill Your church with such disciples again!

Concluding Activities

Conclude with a brief prayer, perhaps asking the Holy Spirit to give strength to our witness by causing our lives to reflect the life of Christ more closely. Then make any necessary announcements and distribute study leaflet 8.

The Church Affirms Gentile Converts as Equals with Jews

Acts 9:32–10:48

Preparing for the Session

Central Focus

The Lord prepared the church to take the Gospel to the Gentile world by teaching Peter and Jewish Christians that they were no longer to regard Gentiles as unclean but as fully eligible for Baptism and membership in the Christian church.

Objectives

That participants, led by the Holy Spirit, will

1. understand that God accepts into His church on an equal basis people of all races and ethnic backgrounds;

2. earnestly seek to rid themselves of all prejudice and feelings of superiority over people on the basis of gender, economic or social class, or race or ethnic derivation;

3. welcome into the church all those in whom the Holy Spirit works faith through the Gospel.

Notes for the small-group leaders: Lesson notes and other materials you will need begin on page 70.

Session Plan

Worship

Begin the session with the hymn printed in the study leaflet and the devotion below. Hymn accompaniments are available in denominational hymnals, such as *Lutheran Worship* (refer to hymnal index). Note: Concordia Publishing House has available *Every Voice a Song*, a 9-CD set of organ accompaniments for 180 hymns and liturgy. All the initial worship hymns in the LifeLight courses are included in this resource. It's especially helpful for mission congregations and small parishes. See the list of study resources on page 7.

Devotion

It seems to be a typical Sunday morning. The church begins to fill with the usual crowd. Friends nod and smile to one another in adjoining pews—those they had not greeted with handshakes and hugs in the narthex before entering the nave. There are some strangers, and they receive a hearty handshake and smiles all around.

Then—whoa! That family is different. Way different! They even look different. They, too, have received handshakes as they entered, but the handshakes were a little stiff. They also had received smiles all around, but the smiles seemed a little forced. The impression might have been given that "of course we welcome you . . . but wouldn't you feel more comfortable with other people more like yourselves?"

Prejudice is hard to shake. It can become a part of our being as we are growing up, and to deny the feelings we have is hard. We may try hard to struggle against such feelings, knowing that we shouldn't have them—yet have them we do.

What can we do about such feelings? First we can acknowledge them to God as sinful attitudes, seek His forgiveness, and ask Him to remove them from us. Second, we can take in His Word even more deeply, knowing that the Gospel can change us from the heart outward.

The Scriptures can be so helpful because they are written about—and written for—real people—people like Peter, who also had to deal with prejudice. His prejudice was not easy for him to deal with, either. God Himself had to change Peter's attitude. And He did.

The Lord can change our attitudes too. You can count on it.

Close with the prayer in the study leaflet.

Lecture Presentation

1 The Door Stays Open in Judea and Samaria (9:32–43)

Verses 32–35—Lydda was a little town on the road from Jerusalem to the seaport town of Joppa.

While walking through the town, Peter came upon a man who had been paralyzed for eight years. Prompted by the Spirit, Peter found out the man's name and, standing before him, said: "Aeneas, . . . Jesus Christ heals you. Get up and take care of your mat." Immediately, not through some gradual process, Aeneas was completely healed, not by Peter but by Jesus Christ. Peter's choice of words makes that absolutely clear.

Luke says nothing more about Aeneas. Rather, he wants us to know about the results of this seal the Lord had just set upon Peter's teaching and preaching. We presume Aeneas came to faith along with the majority (Luke's "all") of those living in this part of Judea.

Verses 36–38—Nine miles from Lydda, in Joppa, was a widowed woman named Tabitha, known in the community by her Greek name, Dorcas, both names meaning a "gazelle doe," a symbol of grace and beauty. Whether she was physically beautiful or not, Luke reports she had another beauty that endeared her to the members of this young congregation—she "was always doing good" (v. 36). Her faith was plainly visible in her actions.

When Dorcas suddenly became sick and died, the believers made no request of Peter but to come. They knew the apostles did not perform miracles on their own, but only when prompted to do so by the Holy Spirit. However, they could hope and trust in the Lord's boundless grace, couldn't they?

Verses 39–40—Genuinely sobbing at their loss, the widows show Peter the clothing Dorcas had made as acts of love for them. Peter was deeply affected, but up to this point had had no indication from the Lord as to why he was there. This is why he ordered everyone from the room, dropped to his knees, and prayed. And then he knew. Acting on the Lord's word, Peter simply and quietly said: "Tabitha, get up"—and the Lord returned her soul to her body and gave hearing to her ears.

Verse 41—Peter opened the door and called everyone into the room "and presented her to them alive." How simply and calmly, and with such an annoying scarcity of words, the sacred writers so often record the most dramatic and stupendous of events!

Verse 42—Hearing about the miracle opened the door for questions, and questions brought answers, and answers were followed by teaching. And the Holy Spirit brought many to faith in Christ. This was the purpose of such extraordinary signs in the days of the apostles.

Verse 43—Why is Luke so specific about where Peter stayed while in Joppa? Because he wants us to take note of something. A crack was beginning to develop in Peter's rigid Jewish background. Simon, the believer whose hospitality Peter accepted, made his living tanning animal hides. Not too long before, Peter would never have set foot in Simon's home, for Simon's occupation made him ceremonially unclean in Jewish eyes. Peter disregarded these Jewish scruples and lived in Simon's home during his entire stay in Joppa. Peter didn't know it yet, but very soon that crack would break wide open.

To avoid some possible misunderstandings, let's take a brief moment to talk about the signs and wonders and miracles performed in the early church. First, it is very clear that none of the apostles and evangelists decided to perform these events on their own. They had nothing to do with choosing whom, how, where, or when. All of this was and still is the Spirit's business. Second, miracles and signs of themselves do not work or create faith. They are the seals of the truth of the Word and validate its power. As such they become an avenue used by the Holy Spirit in creating faith.

Since the Gospel had not yet been written, the Spirit used those miracles to attest to the truth of the apostles' teaching and preaching. That same Spirit inspired the written Gospel record so that those miracles could serve us in the same way today. There is no need for new seals.

2 It's Time to Open Our Door (10:1–7)

The great question that the Lord compelled Peter and the church to face in preparation for Saul's going was whether the way into the Christian church was to be only through Judaism and the synagogue. Or was it possible for believers to be added to the church directly by faith and Baptism alone, whatever their ethnic or religious background? Those early Christians needed some outside help to arrive at God's answer to that important question. And the Lord arranged for that.

Verses 1–2—Some 30 or so miles to the north of Joppa in the newly built town of Caesarea lived a Roman army officer named Cornelius. It was probably the summer of A.D. 38. This Roman officer was a Gentile, but he believed in the God of Israel and respected and attempted to live according to the ethical and moral teachings of Judaism. Such Gentiles are often referred to as "God-fearers" in the New Testament.

This Roman officer was still considered a Gentile by the Jews. But also like the Ethiopian eunuch, Cornelius was well studied in the Scriptures before his conversion. This is an important point, for it prepared them to receive Jesus as the Messiah promised in the Old Testament.

Cornelius shared his faith with his family, and they joined him in that faith. And, finally, Cornelius's faith was alive and well, made plainly visible by the way in which he used his wealth and by his devotion to prayer.

Verses 3–6—It was three o'clock in the afternoon, and Cornelius was praying, perhaps, for a greater understanding of the God he now loved. Suddenly, unexpectedly, his prayer was answered. An angel gave him clear instructions: "Send men to Joppa to bring back a man named Simon who is called Peter. He is staying with Simon the tanner, whose house is by the sea."

Verses 7–8—Cornelius made not a moment's hesitation. He called three servants and fellow believers and sent them on their way to Joppa.

Note carefully again. The Lord could have used the angel to bring the Good News of the Gospel to Cornelius, but *He did not*. Why? Because at the time of His ascension, Jesus gave that task to us, His people. He has chosen to speak the Gospel to people only through other people (believers)—not through angels or any other heavenly being—not even through Christ Himself. The Lord has not changed that principle, and He will not. He has deliberately left that exciting responsibility to us. One of our earnest daily prayers ought to be that the Spirit would give us "opportunity eyes" so that we may "make the most of every opportunity" (Colossians 4:5) He prepares for us to speak the Gospel.

3 Peter Receives Preparatory Schooling (10:9–23a)

Verses 9–13—In Peter's God-given vision, God Himself was abolishing the old Mosaic commands (Leviticus 11; Deuteronomy 14) regarding clean and unclean animals and food. The Lord had given those commands to emphasize that Israel was to be a distinctive people, set apart from all other peoples, through whom the Savior would come into the world. Now the Savior had come, and these laws were no longer needed.

Verse 14—Still, the abolishing of these laws was a radical change indeed, as Peter's reply clearly indicates. "Surely not, Lord! … I have never eaten anything impure or unclean." The crack was still only a crack! Verse 15—Then Peter's unbelieving ears heard, "Do not call anything impure that God has made clean." Verse 16—Three times the lesson was repeated.

Verse 17—While Peter wondered what in the world was the Lord's purpose in all that, the practical application of what he had just learned stood at the front gate. Verses 19–20—The Holy Spirit told Peter about the three men outside the gate and then told Peter not to hesitate to go with them "for I have sent them."

Verse 22—A shiver of excitement must have run through Peter as he heard that Cornelius was eagerly waiting to hear what he had to say. Now it was all beginning to make sense. The Lord had chosen him to officially and publicly bring Christ to the first "ends of the earth" people and to welcome them into Christ's church. Peter probably didn't sleep much that night!

4 Purpose of the Schooling Made Crystal Clear (10:23b–33)

Verses 23–26—Cornelius was concerned that his close friends and relatives also hear the message from God's appointed messenger. Verses 27–29—Without hesitation Peter told his Gentile audience why he, a Jew, was standing in front of them and was comfortable doing so. "God has shown me that I should not call any man impure." Verses 30–33—Cornelius tells the audience of his vision from God.

5 The Gospel Preached to the First "Ends of the Earth" Audience (10:34–43)

With the Spirit's power Peter preached to his Gentile

audience. He reviewed important history that those listening already knew, centering on Jesus of Nazareth. But the listeners had only *heard* of this history—the apostles were eyewitnesses. Christ's selected ones were also eyewitnesses of His crucifixion and, most important of all, of His resurrection, for they "ate and drank with Him after He rose from the dead" (v. 41). Jesus commanded them to preach this Good News, for He is the Judge before whom all peoples, whether living or dead, will stand and be judged. Every one who believes in Him, no matter who he or she is or where he or she lives, receives the great gift of forgiveness and eternal life.

6 The Church Is One and for All— Beyond Dispute (10:44–48)

Verse 44—Before Peter finished his sermon, the Holy Spirit came (fell) on all who were listening in an outward, visible manner. Verses 45–46—They began to speak in other human languages. The Lord dramatically demonstrated by this gift that He had broken down the wall of separation. They, as Gentiles, were no longer strangers and aliens, but fellow citizens with God's people and members of God's household (Ephesians 2:19).

Verse 47—The six Jewish believers who had come with Peter couldn't believe their eyes and ears. But the same Spirit was working in their hearts and minds, for their astonishment did not lead to rejection but acceptance. This is evidenced by the fact that they raised no objection when Peter asked if there was any reason why these new believers should not be baptized.

Verse 48—The Sacrament of Baptism administered on these new Gentile converts is the decisive act that admitted these Gentiles into the Christian church. No intermediary route was necessary. In Holy Baptism their faith was sealed, their forgiveness affirmed, their deliverance from death and the devil guaranteed, and eternal life assured.

Peter gladly accepted the hospitality of Cornelius and stayed with him for a few days. An old dog *can* learn new tricks, especially when the Lord is doing the teaching! Without any scruples or hesitation, Peter sat at Cornelius's table and ate, maybe for the first time in his life, Gentile food.

The final great door to "the ends of the earth" was open. Saul would confidently walk through that door, and the great harvest throughout the world—including us, praise the Lord!—began and will continue until Christ returns. Though it may not always appear so, the holy Christian church today is one and is, beyond all dispute, for all! The same Word, the same Lord, the same Holy Spirit is ours. Let us be up and doing while it is day!

Concluding Activities

Speak a brief prayer, perhaps for deliverance from all prejudice and sinful feelings of superiority over others. Then make any necessary announcements and distribute study leaflet 9.

The Church Thrives Despite Persecution

Acts 11–12

Preparing for the Session

Central Focus

The mission to the Gentiles thrives; Peter successfully explains his Baptism of the Gentile Cornelius and his household, and missionaries establish a largely Gentile church in Antioch of Syria. Herod Agrippa I kills the apostle James and tries to kill Peter, but is thwarted and dies.

Objectives

That participants, led by the Holy Spirit, will

1. understand more clearly that God watches over and blesses His church as it goes about His work;

2. feel more confident of God's care and protection in times of danger and crisis;

3. respond more generously to the physical needs of others, especially of other Christians;

4. courageously witness for Christ, trusting God to guide and guard them.

Notes for the small-group leaders: Lesson notes and other materials you will need begin on page 73.

Session Plan

Worship

Begin the session with the hymn printed in the study leaflet and the devotion below. Hymn accompaniments are available in denominational hymnals, such as *Lutheran Worship* (refer to hymnal index). Note: Concordia Publishing House has available *Every Voice a Song,* a 9-CD set of organ accompaniments for 180 hymns and liturgy. All the initial worship hymns in the LifeLight courses are included in this resource. It's espe-cially helpful for mission congregations and small parishes. See the list of study resources on page 7.

Devotion

Perhaps you have heard the expression that says some-one "sleeps the sleep of the just." That expression refers to someone who can sleep, and sleep peacefully and soundly, because there is no uneasy conscience to dis-turb him or her. Christians, even though conscious of shortcomings and sins, can sleep with an easy con-science because they know that God has forgiven all sins for the sake of Christ Jesus.

Peter, in our study this week, was one who slept the sleep of the just. Peter also slept the sleep of someone who rests in God, who entrusts himself to God, even in a time of crisis or great danger. Peter was in prison, with every expectation that the next morning might well be his last. And yet he slept peacefully and soundly since he rested himself in the care of God.

You and I can do the same, you know. If we don't, if we toss and turn on our pillows, it is not because we have to. We also are in the hands of the Lord, the same Lord who loves us and who has made us His own in Christ. Instead of counting sheep, we can count—and count on—the gracious blessings of God, who was there for us yesterday and who will be there for us in the morn-ing.

Close with the prayer in the study leaflet.

Lecture Presentation

1 **The Whole Church Learns: Yes, Even the Gentiles! (11:1–18)**

Verses 1–3—Word of what had happened in Caesarea spread through the church like a wildfire. To bring non-Jews, Gentiles, into a full and equal relationship, with Jews entering their homes and eating their food at their tables as Peter had done, was astounding. The ones who appeared to be the most upset were those who insisted that circumcision and other Jewish laws were absolutely essential for membership in the Christian church. There was an open and honest confrontation with Peter and the six brothers from the congregation in Joppa in the presence of the Jerusalem congregation, along with an implied willingness to hear Peter's explanation before passing judgment.

The charge was clearly stated and was extremely serious. It was not so much that Peter ate with Gentiles, but that he dared to set aside (break) the Mosaic regulations when he received the Gentiles directly into the church through Baptism. Everybody waited for Peter's explanation and defense.

Verses 4–14—Peter didn't reprimand his accusers, nor did he argue with them. He remembered His own attitude in this whole matter not more than four or five weeks earlier. Beautifully and carefully he led his hearers through the same schooling he had received from the Lord, telling them the whole story of God's speaking to him and Cornelius.

Then Peter told his hearers how the Spirit practically applied the lesson, equipping him to freely and joyfully walk through the door the Lord was opening for the Gentiles. "And the clincher for me," Peter in effect told his audience, "was that as I started to speak, the Holy Spirit gave those hearers the same gift He gave us at Pentecost. It was obvious that God was accepting these Gentiles on the same footing as He had accepted us."

Verses 15–18—Again, the Holy Spirit was at work in the hearts and minds of each listener. Peter's critics not only dropped the charges completely, but they lifted their voices in praise to the Lord as they accepted "even the Gentiles"! God not only opened the door of the church to the Gentiles, but He succeeded in having the Jewish Christians standing inside the door welcoming those Gentiles coming in and praising Him for bringing them into the church.

The same Holy Spirit is present among us and in us today. He can and does work change, break down barriers, remove prejudices, and effect reconciliation and harmony.

2   First Deliberate Outreach to Gentiles (11:19–21)

Stephen's death and the subsequent persecution led Christians to migrate to scattered cities along the Mediterranean, such as Tyre, Sidon, and Ptolemais; to the island of Cyprus; to the large city of Antioch, the capital of Syria and a future center of Christianity. Everywhere these early, untrained Christians went they talked about the message of God's love in Christ. Jewish Christians, natives of Cyprus and Cyrene, began to seek out pagan Greeks and speak to them about Jesus. Undoubtedly, these Cyprians and Cyrenians had heard what Peter had done in Caesarea and the result of the meeting in Jerusalem, and that was all the incentive they needed.

Verse 21—"And the Lord's hand was with them." The Gentile Greeks came into the holy Christian church directly through Baptism and faith—not by converting to Judaism first. How grateful we ought to be to the Lord for making that great truth so abundantly clear!

3   "The Ends of the Earth" Stage Poised for Launch (11:22–26)

Anxious that these new Gentile believers know that they were fully accepted into the one Christian church, the Jerusalem congregation decided to send their greetings and blessing to these new believers in Antioch. All eyes turned to Barnabas. Not only was he "a good man, full of the Holy Spirit and faith" (v. 24), but he had another qualification that made him just the right person for the job—he was a native-born Cyprian, just as some of those who had taken the Gospel to Antioch were (11:20). All this, of course, was neatly set in motion by God.

Barnabas set out on the long journey to Antioch. Verse 23—God's grace at work through these men produced the rich harvest Barnabas saw. Growth in the church, however large or small, is strictly and solely by the grace of God and the work of the Holy Spirit through the spoken and written Word.

Verse 25—Prompted by the Holy Spirit, Barnabas set out on the trip of a hundred miles or so to find Saul, his close friend. Verse 26—For a full year, they immersed themselves in teaching the Good News about Jesus to "great numbers of people," and the Holy Spirit continued to bring in a large harvest. It was here in Antioch that the word *Christian* was applied to the believers. This word is used two more times in the New Testament—in Acts 26:28 and in 1 Peter 4:16.

4 First "World Relief" Effort (11:27–30)

Among the gifts of the Holy Spirit listed in 1 Corinthians 12 is the gift of prophecy. From what we can gather, the prophets who served in the church at Antioch were Christian teachers to whom the Spirit at times gave special direct communications of events or happenings important for the congregation's consideration. The Holy Spirit moved Agabus and a number of others with the same gift to make the long trip to Antioch to warn about a coming famine.

It is interesting that the Holy Spirit chose this moment to again verify the historical accuracy of Luke's account. Luke has so far not given us any dates. Suddenly he does so by inserting the words "This happened during the reign of Claudius" (v. 28). Claudius ruled the Roman empire from January, A.D. 41, to October, A.D. 54. Roman writers and the great Jewish historian Josephus tell us that crop failures and famine conditions marked much of Claudius's reign.

Verse 29—The disciples began to gather an offering to help the congregations in Judea "each according to his ability." This is a clear demonstration that faith in Christ also produces a change in attitude toward the earthly possessions with which the Christian is blessed by the Lord. And so the gathering of the first "world relief" offering got under way.

5 Satan's Fury Felt Again (12:1–5)

Verse 1—Early in A.D. 41 Emperor Claudius made Herod Agrippa I, a grandson of Herod the Great, king over all Palestine. Jerusalem was his capital, and since his elevation to kingship he had been busy courting the favor of the Jews, especially that of the Pharisees. This was fertile ground for Satan when he was allowed to unleash his fury again. Verse 2—Martyrdom also happened again, only this time it came to one of the apostles. James, the brother of John, was arrested and beheaded. Verse 3—The Sanhedrin were delighted and quickly let Herod know he had their full support. And so Herod stepped up his activities, looking for bigger game.

Unaware of what had happened, Peter was on his way into the city, where he was arrested and thrown into prison. Verses 4–5—Four squads of soldiers were assigned to guard Peter in shifts. Two were to be chained to Peter in the cell, and two were to guard the door. "But the church was earnestly praying to God for him."

6 Iron Bars Do Not a Prison Make (12:6–17)

Verse 6—Luke takes us to what, humanly speaking, would have been Peter's last night on earth. Yet Peter slept like a baby! How eloquently and beautifully this sleep testified that "to live is Christ and to die is gain" (Philippians 1:21)!

Verses 7–11—Luke goes into great detail about the actual escape, having heard exactly what happened from Peter himself some time later.

Verses 12–14—The street on which the angel left Peter wasn't an accidental choice, for it led him to a home where some of his close friends lived. Peter went to the door of the courtyard and knocked.

We can imagine what was going on inside that house. Remember, it was probably two o'clock in the morning. The small group of Christians had been praying nonstop since Peter's imprisonment. All hope of an answer from the Lord was almost gone. Suddenly, there was a knock at the door.

Luke employs his great sense of humor to teach us a lesson or two as he describes in detail what follows. Rhoda immediately recognized the voice that spoke to her from the other side of the door. She believed her ears. She was so excited and happy that she forgot to unlock the door! Instead she burst back into the room she had just left and shouted, "Peter is at the door!"

Verse 15—They looked at her as if she were crazy and told her so. Undeterred, certain her ears did not deceive her, she kept yelling: "I'm not crazy—Peter is here!" But the others had convinced themselves that Peter was already dead and that his guardian angel was standing outside to tell them the sad news.

After praying for Peter's deliverance for hours, the thought that God might answer their prayers and free Peter at this late hour seemed simply unbelievable to them. How many of us are Rhodas, and how many are all too often like the rest of the praying group? How often do we pray not really expecting the Lord to answer, just going through the motions? And even when we pray and plead earnestly, do we see or recognize the answer when it comes? Luke's humorous recounting of the details makes us laugh, and maybe the Lord laughs with us, understanding and forgiving our often little faith.

Verse 16—In the meantime, Peter stood patiently knocking at the door. Still convinced that Rhoda was dreaming, but knowing now the knocking was not coming from any soldiers of Herod, they finally unlocked the door. To their astonishment there stood Peter alive and well! Verse 17—Quickly Peter quieted them so he could tell them how the Lord freed him. He also gave directions for them to tell James and the rest of the congregation. (This would be Jesus' brother James, who was the leader of the Jerusalem congregation.) And then Peter left the city for a while—where, Luke simply does not say.

7 The Lord Abruptly Blows Out the Fury (12:18–23)

Shortly after Herod sent for Peter and found out there was no Peter to bring, he ordered the guards executed. He didn't know it, but the Lord was about to bring Herod's three-year rule and his life to an abrupt and horrible end. And so it happened, and the time of peace returned again.

8 The Countdown Begins (12:24–25)

This is the way the histories of persecutions always end. Herod perished, the Word just grew and grew and grew in more and more hearts.

Their mission was finished, the offering had been delivered for distribution to those in need. Saul and Barnabas, taking Mark with them, started out on the long trip back to Antioch. How much they had to talk about! Since peace had come again, maybe they had even spent some time with Peter. One thing they were not aware of—the countdown for their launch "to the ends of the earth" had begun.

Concluding Activities

Thank participants for taking part in this LifeLight course and invite them to take part in the next LifeLight course. Encourage them to bring someone else with them. Speak a brief prayer, perhaps thanking God for the blessings received in this LifeLight course. Then distribute study leaflet 1 for any subsequent LifeLight course.

Small-Group Leaders Material

The Church Is Prepared for Pentecost

Acts 1

Preparing for the Session

Central Focus

As we begin this study of Acts, we are introduced to its author, Luke; we hear Jesus' final instructions to His disciples before He ascends into heaven; and we observe the manner by which the ranks of the 12 apostles are restored after the defection of Judas.

Objectives

That participants, led by the Holy Spirit, will

1. understand the purpose of this book and its relationship to Luke's Gospel;

2. realize the importance of proclaiming the Gospel to the world as the central task of Christians and the reason why the world continues to exist;

3. desire to make sharing the Gospel with others a primary goal of their lives;

4. seek opportunities to pray and worship together with fellow Christians as a means of strengthening themselves as witnesses for Jesus.

Small-Group Discussion Helps

Day 1 • Acts 1:1–5

1. Luke, the author of Acts, provides glimpses of the great moments and personalities involved in the growth of the early church. Drawing on records of the churches at Jerusalem, Caesarea, and Antioch, Luke shows the expansion of Christianity in Jerusalem (Acts 1:1–6:7), through Palestine and Samaria (6:8–9:31), to Antioch (9:32–12:24). Later in Acts (chapters 16–28), Luke gives a firsthand account of events. His message: The Gospel is for everyone. (a) Luke refers to his first book, the Gospel according to Luke, where he describes all that Jesus *began* to do and teach. (b) Luke's sequel, the Acts of the Apostles, will describe Jesus' *ongoing*

work through His people as they are empowered by the Holy Spirit to spread the Gospel "to the ends of the earth."

2. Luke records the power of the Spirit, sent by the resurrected Christ, alive in Christ's people. He shows how the Word spreads and grows. The number of disciples increases. The Holy Spirit strengthens the church.

3. As time permits, allow participants to share their reasons for their responses.

4. (a) Luke was a careful researcher and organizer. He investigated the details of Jesus' life and work and wrote an "orderly account" of what he learned. This shows that Luke was a scholar—educated and trained. (b) Luke was a doctor, Paul's "dear friend." (c) Paul calls Luke a fellow worker, one who accompanied and assisted the apostle on his missionary travels. (d) Luke was among Paul's most loyal companions, one who stood by the apostle even during the dark days of his imprisonment and approaching death.

Day 2 • Acts 1:6–8

5. Jesus and His disciples were probably walking together toward the mount of ascension. It was their last opportunity to talk together. The disciples brought up a subject obviously important and urgent to them: They were concerned about an earthly kingdom. Political power and status seemed to be priorities, still, for them. Like other Jews, they saw their nation as special and looked forward to the day when God would break in and intervene to make them world sovereigns.

6. *For personal reflection. Sharing optional.* All kinds of concerns no doubt will surface, probably including worries about health, money, and the future. Help participants to see that as we rely on the comfort of Jesus' resurrection and speak about "what Jesus means to me" (especially as He enters into our "earthly" worries and concerns), we do serve as His witnesses.

7. Disciples of Jesus will continue His work in ever-widening circles until everyone, to the ends of the earth, has heard the message of His love. Until that happens, the work goes on.

8. **Challenge question.** Do not ask for a response to this question.

Day 3 • Acts 1:9–11

9. The single reason for the continuation of time and history after Christ's ascension is that all people throughout the world will hear about God's love for them in Christ and by the Spirit's power become members of the holy Christian church. Jesus returned to heaven to assume His lordship for the church. The visible church on earth is His body, active in continuing His work. Christ, as true man, is not only present everywhere, but also now fully exercises His divine power over the whole universe. But in a very special way He is with us and lives *within* His people and sends His Spirit to strengthen us to witness to all people.

Day 4 • Acts 1:12–14

10. Perhaps being together gave Jesus' followers, friends, and relatives courage and helped them feel less lonely. Perhaps they sensed their need for one another—just as we need to be with others when we've lost someone we love. Prayer links them with their beloved Lord.

11. Earlier (v. 4) Jesus had told the disciples not to leave Jerusalem. They accepted His authority now even when He was gone. They stayed and waited, as He had commanded.

12. At first Jesus' brothers did not believe that He was the Messiah. But now they are mentioned among the believers (v. 14). The logical conclusion is that they had experienced Jesus' resurrection and had come to faith. Perhaps Jesus' brothers saw Him alive during one of His post-Easter appearances.

13. (a) *For personal reflection. Sharing optional.* Together Christians wait for answers to prayer, for direction in making decisions and taking action, for inner peace. (b) Encourage participants to share their experiences with prayer groups, support groups, and Bible-discussion groups. (Perhaps they have been involved with LifeLight for some time.) Highlight the strength and encouragement Christians experience as they pray together. Focus on the benefits and blessings of Christian fellowship, such as spiritual growth, becoming more aware of God's grace, and being willing to admit sins and experience forgiveness.

Day 5 • Acts 1:15–26

14. Perhaps Peter was anxious to be up and doing something practical. He reminded the other believers that the Scripture had been fulfilled regarding what happened to Judas. Now he pointed out that the Scriptures also called for Judas to be replaced.

15. Peter clearly used the Scripture to guide the selection of Judas's replacement (v. 20). Then the church called upon God in prayer, asking Him to guide the selection (v. 24). Similarly we need to look for direction to Scripture and ask for God's guidance as we read and as we seek to carry out His will.

16. Nominees had to be witnesses to Jesus' resurrection and a part of the group traveling with Jesus throughout His ministry.

17. Proverbs 16:33 assures us that Matthias's selection was not a matter of chance but that the Lord Himself had chosen Matthias, just as Jesus had personally chosen the other disciples.

18. (a) That such a small group of people (120) should carry the Gospel so far (Rome is 1,500 miles distant from Jerusalem) in such a short time (30 years) is amazing, considering the state of communication and travel at that time. Christianity spread quickly after Pentecost. Although persecuted by the greatest power in the world, Christianity would conquer Rome itself a little more than two centuries later. The power of the Spirit was at work through a small group of believers to take the Gospel to the ends of the earth, just as Jesus had said (v. 8). (b) Encourage participants to share their feelings and experiences. It is not always easy to witness for Jesus. The world is hostile to the Gospel. We may be harassed, ridiculed, ignored, or shunned. We may feel powerless when faced with overwhelming opposition. Yet each Christian's witness is crucial. Faith spreads, by the power of the Spirit in the Word, through the interrelatedness of human beings—one life touching another. Encourage everyone in your group to name a person whose witness in word and action has been a profound influence.

19. Ask volunteers to share the verse or section most meaningful to them. Urge them to explain reasons for their selections, but don't force the sharing.

The Church Is Empowered by the Holy Spirit

Acts 2:1–41

Preparing for the Session

Central Focus

On Pentecost Day the Holy Spirit came upon Jesus' followers, as Jesus had promised and as Joel and John the Baptist had prophesied, drawing a large crowd from many nations around them. Peter proclaimed the Gospel to this crowd by an inspired sermon, and the result was that 3,000 people were moved by the Spirit to repentance and to faith in Jesus as the Messiah.

Objectives

That participants, led by the Holy Spirit, will

1. realize that the events of Pentecost Day were in fulfillment of prophecy and of Jesus' promise;

2. understand that God gives the gift of the Holy Spirit to all believers through Holy Baptism;

3. become more aware of and confident in the Holy Spirit's presence in them;

4. desire to share the Gospel with others;

5. by repentance and faith reclaim the baptismal gifts each day and begin again to live a new life of holiness and righteousness by the Spirit's power.

Small-Group Discussion Helps

Day 1 • Acts 2:1–13

1. (a) Jesus promised to send the Holy Spirit to the disciples (Luke 24:49; Matthew 3:11; Luke 3:16). He commanded that they wait in Jerusalem for the fulfillment of His promise. On the day of Pentecost the city was surely crowded with people from all parts of Palestine and the Mediterranean world. Pentecost, also called the Festival of Weeks or the Feast of Harvest, was similar to the American/Canadian Thanksgiving Day. It was an

agricultural festival celebrated seven weeks after the harvest began. The firstfruits of the wheat harvest were presented to God. Crowds were swarming to the temple to watch the priests wave the loaves and sacrifice the lambs in worship to the Lord, who had made the harvest possible. All Jewish males were required to worship in Jerusalem that day and were invited to join in an altar dance and song. Surely large, noisy crowds packed the city on that Pentecost, probably May, A.D. 30. (b) The believers were gathered for prayer and fellowship either in the upper room, or (as some commentators suggest) in a room at the temple where they met daily (Luke 24:53). (c) Perhaps, in addition to prayer and praise to God, they encouraged one another by remembering and reviewing the teachings of Jesus. In any event, they were waiting for the fulfillment of Jesus' promise to send the Holy Spirit.

2. (a) The visible signs of the Holy Spirit's presence were the noise like a mighty wind and tongues like fire. The noise surely drew crowds in the city to the place where the disciples were gathered. (b) Fire, in the Old Testament, signified the presence of God. (c) Proof that the Spirit had entered into the believers was their ability to speak languages other than their native tongues (vv. 4, 6, 8). This was not possible without the Spirit's filling them. (What a practical miracle, since witness to the Gospel would require knowledge of many languages!) (d) The purpose of the gift was the witness to what God had done.

3. Each Christian (vv. 3–4) was filled with the Holy Spirit. Each Christian received the gift of language. Peter explains the miracle by quoting Joel's prophecy (vv. 17–21). The inclusiveness of sons and daughters, old and young, men and women is encouraging to everyone. Neither age nor gender limits the indwelling Spirit. Everyone is equipped for witness. Encourage group members to share how they feel about being included in receiving the Spirit and being gifted by the Spirit for service and witness. Discuss ways to open up and increase opportunities for witness within your congregation or community.

4. Participants may need special encouragement in rec-

ognizing and verbalizing the work of the Spirit within them. Admitting that the Spirit lives within is not boasting. It is the Spirit who convicts us of sin, creates repentance and faith, and moves us to witness and service. Remind one another that faith in Christ is the primary evidence of the indwelling Holy Spirit: "no one can say 'Jesus is Lord,' except by the Holy Spirit" (1 Corinthians 12:3). Remind one another that in our Baptism we received the Holy Spirit, who creates and sustains our faith (Acts 2:38–39; 1 Corinthians 6:11).

Day 2 • Acts 2:14–21

5. (a) Words that might be used to describe Peter before Pentecost might include straightforward, confident, sure of himself, and bold (Matthew 16:21–23), cowardly and untruthful (Matthew 26:69–75), impetuous and aggressive (John 18:10–11). (b) Peter approached the crowd courteously and winsomely, yet eagerly and confidently. He appealed to His Jewish audience by quoting Scripture. Only the Spirit could transform a blustering, vacillating fisherman into a powerful preacher who, without preparation, delivered a masterpiece of a sermon!

6. Images of war, urban rioting, violence, murder, and great calamities in nature (volcanoes, hurricanes, etc.) are signs of the end of the world. We see them portrayed almost daily on TV and in our newspapers.

7. The horrors of this present world—and the escalation of these preceding the day of judgment—remind us that Jesus is coming again and that we and all who call on His name will be "saved," will experience "redemption."

Not only will we be saved from eternal wrath and separation from God, but as people "redeemed," bought back from death and hell, we'll enter into the full joy and glory of eternal life with God (Matthew 25:34).

Day 3 • Acts 2:22–36

8. The crucifixion of Jesus is an essential part of the plan of God to save sinners. Peter made this clear to His Jewish listeners who had rejected the idea of a suffering and dying Messiah. He had to help them see the suffering and death of Jesus as a fulfillment of prophecy. At the same time, the Jews had to accept their personal responsibility for Jesus' death and understand their guilt. Jesus says this about His crucifixion: "But I, when I am lifted up from the earth, *will draw all men to Myself*" (John 12:32). Isaiah 53:2–10 is a powerful prophecy of Jesus' suffering and death as God's own substitute, dying to pay for our sin. Peter also quotes Psalm 16:8–11, where David prophesied of Christ and His resurrection.

9. (a) When we understand that Jesus' death on the cross was the payment for our sins, (b) then His resurrection becomes for us the final proof that He is our Savior and that the payment for our sins is complete. Then we are sure of new life in Him now and into all eternity. Encourage volunteers to share their own answers.

Day 4 • Acts 2:37–39

10. Peter's hearers were "cut to the heart." They regretted their rejection of Jesus. They were troubled and convicted. They were eager to know more and were ready to act as they were directed.

11. He tells them to repent and be baptized to receive forgiveness and the gift of the Holy Spirit. Peter calls, invites, urges, and offers the Gospel to all. He is clear, sincere, winsome, and appealing. He speaks the truth in love.

12. In Baptism we all received the gifts of faith, forgiveness, and the benefits of Christ's suffering, death, and resurrection.

13. The main use of this question is for the participants' individual study. Unless someone wants to comment, move on to the next question. (The Romans text is a key to the practical, ongoing meaning of our Baptism.) Scripture assures us that in our Baptism we have died with Christ to sin and that with Him we have been raised to live a new life. Through daily confession and forgiveness we are freed from slavery to sin. We live every day in the grace of God. When we experience God's grace personally, daily, we are patient and forgiving with others. We love, serve, and share the Good News of God's grace with those around us.

Day 5 • Acts 2:40–41

14. (a) God calls sinners through the message concerning Christ. Faith is the gift of the Spirit and comes

through hearing that message. (b) By the power of the Spirit, 3,000 people believed and were baptized that day! Paul Maier remarks: "Not even Jesus' preaching had drawn such a response, at least not in Jerusalem, or there would have been more believers than the lonesome 120 Christians before Pentecost" (*In the Fullness of Time*, New York: Harper Collins, 1991; p. 218).

15. (a) Talk about opportunities at home, on the job, or in the community. Share styles and strategies that members have found effective. (b) Emphasize that the Spirit gives the right words and actions at the right time. (c) Pray together for the Spirit's power and direction. Pray for specific persons or situations.

16. Ask for volunteers to share.

The Church Proclaims the Word with Great Boldness

Acts 2:42–4:31

Preparing for the Session

Central Focus

Boldly, the church—led by the apostles Peter and John—proclaims the Gospel about Jesus to the residents of Jerusalem and courageously defies the orders of the Sanhedrin to stop proclaiming this Gospel.

Objectives

That participants, led by the Holy Spirit, will

1. know that the courage to speak the Gospel boldly comes from the presence of the Holy Spirit within Christians;

2. desire to proclaim the Gospel more boldly in our world today;

3. devote themselves more consistently to the Gospel offered to us in Word and Sacrament;

4. be ready to speak boldly to others about God's love and grace for us in Jesus, the Savior.

Small-Group Discussion Helps

Day 1 • Acts 2:42–47

1. As Matthew 28:20 indicates, the apostles taught people everything that Jesus had taught them. The heart and core of that teaching was the "good news" about Jesus, sent by God to His people, whom they wickedly crucified, and whom God raised from the dead. It's "good news" because it confers forgiveness of sins and the gift of the Holy Spirit to all who repent (turn from their sins) and accept the message of forgiveness won by Christ.

2. As the cited references indicate, "the breaking of bread" often refers to the Lord's Supper. It probably means that here.

3. **Challenge question.** Many miracles were done by the apostles in the early church, but such miracles seem to have become quite infrequent with the end of the apostolic era. This suggests that the Lord gave these signs (and perhaps other powerful signs, such as speaking in other tongues or languages) as a special way of launching the church; sort of an initial liftoff. We see that in the church's earliest days, literally thousands joined in response to the ministry of the apostles. Note Paul's emphasis in 1 Corinthians 13:8 on the temporary nature of such "special" gifts as tongues and the greater importance of Christian love for edifying the church. 2 Corinthians 12:12 and other texts indicate that "signs, wonders and miracles" were connected with the apostles personally.

4. As time permits, allow participants to share reasons for their ranking. The question and sharing of answers is intended to lead participants to sober reflection, mutual encouragement, and to prayer for renewal in the church—beginning with each individual!

5. (a) The Lord brought people to faith in Jesus through the Gospel and added them to the church. This is also affirmed by Isaiah. God's Word brings about the results He intends as surely as does the seed as it responds to His creating power. (b) This truth is surely reassuring to the church today also as we proclaim the Gospel. We are not to be discouraged should our efforts not bring about the results we expect; we can be sure that God's Word will bring people to faith and strengthen believers.

Day 2 • Acts 3:1–10

6. As long as they were permitted to do so, Jewish Christians continued to use the temple in Jerusalem as a place of prayer and also for teaching the Gospel to others. However, as the letter to the Hebrews points out, the purpose of the temple changed for Jewish Christians. They no longer needed to offer the sacrifices for the atonement of sins since they knew that Christ had already atoned for their sins once for all. So, though they continued to use the temple as a house of

prayer, it was no longer needed as a place for sacrifice. In this sense the temple was obsolete and would soon disappear altogether. This temple was destroyed by the Roman army under Titus, who leveled Jerusalem in A.D. 70 during the Jewish War.

7. (a) *Jesus* means "Savior." (b) Christ, the "Anointed One," was anointed (set aside, appointed) by the Holy Spirit (Acts 10:38) to be our Prophet, Priest, and King.

8. "Of Nazareth" points to His human origin. He was born (in Bethlehem) and grew up in a specific place—the town of Nazareth. He died—as humans do. Yet He is also "the author of life"—a statement that can refer only to God Himself. "Without Him nothing was made that has been made" (John 1:3). Jesus, therefore, is in one person "true God, begotten of the Father from eternity, and also true man, born of the Virgin Mary" (Explanation to the Second Article, Luther's Small Catechism, CPH, 1986). Our Savior had to be true man so that, as a true human being, He might be able to take our place under God's Law and die for our guilt, for our failure to keep God's Law. He had to be true God so that He could keep that Law perfectly and so that His suffering and death might be a sufficient ransom for all people. If time permits, share this commentary by Luther on the practical value for us of this Word of God:

"We Christians must know that if God is not also in the balance, and gives the weight, we sink to the bottom with our scale. By this I mean: If it were not to be said, God has died for us, but only a man, we should be lost. But if 'God's death' and 'God died' lie in the scale of the balance, then He sinks down, and we rise up as a light, empty scale. But indeed He can also rise again or leap out of the scale; yet He could not sit in the scale unless He became a man like us, so that it could be said: 'God died,' 'God's passion,' 'God's blood,' 'God's death.' For in His nature God cannot die; but now that God and man are united in one person, it is correctly called God's death, when the man dies who is one thing or one person with God" (*Concordia Triglotta*, pp. 1029–31).

9. *For personal reflection. Sharing optional.* Perhaps some participants will want to tell about some great—or small—unexpected blessing they received and to express their thanks and praise to God for that blessing.

10. God does give us golden opportunities to tell others about His grace and love through Jesus. Encourage par-

ticipants to share these evidences of God's grace from their own lives with others in their discussion group.

Day 3 • Acts 3:11–26

11. (a) In both sermons, Peter accuses the hearers of disowning and of killing the "Righteous One" God sent. (b) God raised His Son from the dead and raised Him to His own right hand (glorified Him). (c) We receive forgiveness when we repent (turn from sin and in faith accept Christ).

12. Encourage volunteers to share their choices and explain their reasons.

13. As time permits, encourage and allow volunteers to share.

14. All the Bible texts support the summary statement. "I am with you always" (Matthew 28:20) refers to the whole Christ, the God-man who spoke these words to the disciples as they saw Him, physically resurrected, standing in their midst. At the ascension, Jesus withdrew His visible presence from them. But according to His promise He, the God-man, was still present with them, although now invisibly. Acts 1:11 and Revelation 1:7 affirm that at the Last Day Jesus will visibly appear and thus "come back in the same way you have seen Him go." The Ephesians text portrays the Christ, "raised . . . from the dead" (obviously referring to His human nature), as the God-man who now rules over everything and who "fills everything in every way." From eternity the Son of God was everywhere present. But now, as the Colossians text affirms, "in Christ all the fullness of the Deity lives in bodily form" and He is present with us also according to His human nature. The divine and the human natures are united in Jesus Christ. The personal union, begun when He became man (incarnation), continues forever.

Day 4 • Acts 4:1–22

15. "They were greatly disturbed," (v. 2) tells the attitude of the Jewish leaders and the Sanhedrin, who were especially hostile to the apostles because the doctrine of "the resurrection of the dead," which contradicted one of their basic beliefs. They wanted to keep peace with Rome in order to protect their own status.

16. Note these similarities: Peter courageously explains a miracle (earlier, the miracle of Pentecost, now the miracle of healing the lame man), convicts them of their responsibility for Jesus' death, witnesses to the resurrection, points to Christ as the one Savior, and quotes Old Testament prophecy.

17. The miracle cannot be denied. The people were all praising God for the miracle. Although the members of the Sanhedrin are embarrassed by the healed man and annoyed because they recognize Peter and John as part of the movement they had tried to destroy, they are helpless to do more than bluster and threaten.

18. (a) As much as time permits, dig deeply into this question. It addresses a pervading and often subtle works-righteousness that tempts us all. The Romans and Galatians texts contrast salvation by grace through faith with Israel's (and many "good church people's") seeking to base their relationship with God on keeping the Law—an effort doomed to failure since no one is able to, in fact, keep the Law perfectly, as the Law demands.

(b) As time permits, encourage sharing. Important in any response to a works-righteousness statement is the responder's acknowledgment that he or she, too, is tempted to rely on his or her own "goodness." Isn't it wonderful that we don't have to justify ourselves before God—that Jesus really did it all for us?

19. Again, encourage sharing as time permits.

20. God requires us to submit to the governing authorities, but when these authorities command what is clearly contrary to God, we are bound to obey our Lord alone.

....

Day 5 • Acts 4:23–31

21. **Challenge question.** If time is running short, you may want to pass over this question. Another option would be to have a volunteer lead the group in the prayer he or she has written.

22. "Nations"—Gentiles, particularly the Roman nation. "Peoples"—the people of Israel. "Kings of the earth"—Herod. "Rulers"—Pontius Pilate. "Anointed One"— Jesus Christ.

23. (a) Participants will no doubt mention places in the world today where Christians still face outright persecution. More subtle are such threats as peer pressure at the workplace to "go along with the gang," the deadening effect of anti-Christian and sub-Christian "entertainment" on TV and in other popular media, and advocacy groups that espouse anti-Christian causes.

(b) As time permits, encourage but do not pressure volunteers to share. Focus discussion on scary or difficult situations where members find it difficult to witness, for example, to a reluctant spouse, adult children, hostile neighbors, members of sects. Pray together for courage and the Spirit's power.

(c) Answers will vary.

24. Our congregations and our larger church body also would be a more effective corporate witness to the Gospel if we spoke with greater boldness than we do. Encourage participants to share their specific ideas on how to do so. Both in our own society and in societies around the world such boldness would provide a more powerful witness through word and deed. Oh, that we might ask and be ready to receive this greater boldness!

25. Lead a brief prayer, asking for this boldness.

The Church Meets Both Internal and External Challenges

Acts 4:32–5:42

Preparing for the Session

Central Focus

Strengthened and blessed with a wonderful unity centered in the Gospel, the church successfully meets a challenge from within raised by hypocrisy and a challenge from without raised by the threats of the Jewish leaders.

Objectives

That participants, led by the Holy Spirit, will

1. be more aware of the seriousness of the sin of hypocrisy;

2. be willing to share their own blessings in meeting the needs of other Christians;

3. show courage in witnessing boldly for Jesus.

Small-Group Discussion Helps

Day 1 • Acts 4:32–37

1. The believers' priorities are clear. They gave top priority to God's Word and their witness to Christ's resurrection. They viewed their personal possessions as resources for the common good. They used them to care for one another. Their sharing was spontaneous, not legislated. In one accord in word and witness, they felt it unthinkable that some could have too much while others had too little. How different in today's modern society where individualism, competition, and the acquisition of material goods are top priorities.

2. All believers received the Holy Spirit. The Spirit living within the hearts of believers affected their choices.

3. Barnabas must have made quite an impression on the apostles as evidenced by the name change. Surely he lived up to his nickname, "Son of Encouragement,"

in more than this one example of unselfishness (4:36–37). In addition to being unselfish, he was helpful, encouraging, a mediator, and an advocate (9:26–28). He was good, full of the Spirit, and faithful (11:19–30), consecrated by the Spirit (13:1–3), a witness to the Gospel (14:21–28), forgiving and accepting, as seen in the case of John Mark (15:36–41).

4. (a) Urge participants to name their "Barnabas." Hopefully, your LifeLight study has developed relationships that are encouraging and supportive. (b) When the Spirit of Christ lives within Christians, Jesus is visible. Jesus' love, care, concern, and forgiveness are expressed through believers within the context of relationships. They give unselfishly of their time and attention. They pray together. They urge repentance and assure forgiveness. They share God's Word. They share spiritual truths they've learned on their own personal journeys. They are the "training wheels" for others. At the same time they are aware of physical and emotional needs and are ready to help when needed. Encourage group members to share specifically how others have helped them. (c) As a group, think of ways to encourage others on their spiritual journey. Point out that an encourager is accepting and affirming, positive and supportive. They contrast with discouragers, who are critical and negative, often censoring and rejecting others. Underscore our common neediness and God's amazing grace.

Day 2 • Acts 5:1–11

5. (a) The sharing of personal property was strictly voluntary. Property was made available as needed. The sharing was designed to meet needs, not equalize everyone economically. Therefore, Ananias and Sapphira would not have been criticized for the size of their offering—their sin was pretending they had given it all, the full amount of the sale. (b) Apparently, Ananias and Sapphira tried to win praise through deception. Their offering may have looked good "on the books," but God looks upon the heart. He sees what others cannot see.

6. Peter was giving Sapphira an opportunity to tell the truth. She did not have to continue in the sin she and Ananias had devised. She could have repented and sought forgiveness. If she had, she probably would not have paid the same penalty as her husband. She might have been forgiven and continued her life within the Christian community.

7. (a) Ananias and Sapphira tried to deceive the Holy Spirit. That couldn't be done. (b) Keep in mind that the scheme of Ananias and Sapphira had been deliberate, their action had been public, and the consequences of their action would have had a far-reaching effect on a brand new, struggling church. The penalty may seem harsh to us, but that probably says more about us than it does about God's punishment. Finally, all sin is worthy of death (Romans 6:23).

Day 3 • Acts 5:12–16

8. (a) Jesus' promise that such miraculous signs would be done through the apostles was being fulfilled. The disciples were given the miraculous power through the indwelling Christ. Jesus and His healing power was alive within them—a further proof of the resurrection. The apostles' healing was an extension of Jesus' healing. Also, these signs caused people to pay attention to the message the apostles spoke. (b) The believers defied the Sanhedrin. Daily they met openly in an area of the temple accommodating thousands. They were unafraid of the consequences. They chose to obey God rather than men. (c) Perhaps the hangers-on were scared away by what happened to Ananias and Sapphira. It seems none of them joined just to climb on the bandwagon or enjoy the reputation of those attached to a popular movement. (d) The Spirit was working powerfully, creating faith that spread from person to person to person. (e) Move to the next question unless someone wants to speak.

9. (a) Women waited with the others in Jerusalem. They received the gift of the Holy Spirit at Pentecost. They were part of the learning, worshiping fellowship. As believers, they were also called to be witnesses for the risen Christ. Women in the early Christian church were taught and treated as partners in the task of carrying the Gospel into the world. The Gospel is inclusive. Everyone is called to repentance and faith. All are gifted with the Spirit and made witnesses for Jesus. Grace alone, not rank, gender, or status, links us to Him. (b) This is encouraging to both women and men. As partners, they are supported by one another's unique strengths and gifts.

Day 4 • Acts 5:17–26

10. We might imagine that these Christians might have momentarily, at least, experienced the normal human emotions of fear or sorrow at such news. However, previous experiences had surely taught them to respond with faith and prayer (4:23–31).

11. Upon their release they obeyed the angel's direction and went directly to the temple to resume teaching and witnessing (5:21). Their arrest could have sapped their courage. Fear of what the authorities could do to them might have shut their mouths. But that did not happen. They obeyed God first.

12. God intervenes. God has His way. The miraculous release from jail, plus the miraculous courage, eloquence, power, and obedience shown by the apostles, shows that the church is the Lord's and is not a human institution.

13. (a) They were released to "tell the people the full message of this new life" (v. 20). Their release also demonstrated to the Jewish leaders that God was behind the ministry of the apostles. (b) Help participants to see that every Christian has been released from sin, from death, and from the power of the devil through Christ's death and resurrection. Affirm one another in your purpose as witnesses to the Gospel.

Day 5 • Acts 5:27–42

14. (a) The high priest ignored the miraculous release of the apostles from jail. Uppermost on his agenda was that the apostles had defied his authority and that they were trying to make the Sanhedrin responsible for Jesus' death. The high priest would have none of it. The apostles had to be stopped! (b) Peter, however, had his own agenda. He would witness to Jesus' victorious resurrection after His death; he would call the Sanhedrin to repentance and forgiveness; he would give credit to the Holy Spirit.

15. The Sanhedrin were deeply troubled by Peter's words. But instead of acknowledging their sin, they were furious and ready to murder the apostles. They closed their eyes to the evidence of the miracles, the large number of converts, the generosity, and the joy of the believers. Perhaps they refused to believe because it would mean that they would have to give up a religion centered on themselves. In contrast, those who responded to Peter in 2:37 seem to have emptied themselves of their pride and stood helpless and open to the Holy Spirit. The self-righteousness of the Sanhedrin made it difficult, if not impossible, for them to repent.

16. Encourage participants to share their definitions of faith. Faith is trust in the forgiveness of sins earned for us by Christ. Faith is the gift of the Holy Spirit, who comes to us through Word and Sacraments. (b) As we feed on God's Word—especially the message of His forgiveness in Christ—our faith continues to grow. Cut off from that source of power, our faith withers and dies. This applies to individuals and to congregations. A church bold in its witness is a learning, growing, worshiping church. Explore with your group ways to promote and increase involvement in congregational worship and Bible study.

17. Gamaliel was the most famous Jewish teacher of his time; he was respected, loved, and perhaps kindlier than others on the Sanhedrin. His cool head seems to have made him a friend of the apostles. Yet he had the same evidence as others who already believed. Why didn't he repent and believe too? Why didn't he urge others to do the same? Was he a fence sitter?

18. Encourage volunteers to share their answers.

The Church Has Its First Martyr

Acts 6–7

Preparing for the Session

Central Focus

To allow the apostles to concentrate on their spiritual duties, the church selects seven helpers or deacons. One of them, Stephen, becomes the first Christian to give the ultimate witness to his faith—by dying because of it.

Objectives

That participants, led by the Holy Spirit, will

1. understand a God-pleasing manner of resolving disputes with fellow Christians;

2. realize that a consistent witness to Jesus may draw the opposition of unbelievers;

3. be confident of God's guidance and sustaining presence when our witness meets with hostility;

4. be courageous and have trust in God in witnessing to Jesus.

Small-Group Discussion Helps

Day 1 • Acts 6:1–7

1. (a) The apostles had their priorities straight. They knew their first concern was prayer and preaching (vv. 2, 4). (b) They had confidence in others, affirming the diversity of gifts within the church. Perhaps the most significant feature of their problem-solving strategy is the way they involved the whole body in the decision-making process (v. 3). This shows the apostles were not self-serving or power-hungry but confident in the Spirit's power alive in their fellow believers. (c) The apostles emphasized, however, that the congregation was to choose men who were "known to be full of the Spirit and wisdom" (v. 3), thus affirming the necessity of spir-

itual qualifications.

2. (a) As long as Christians live in this body and world, they struggle with their sinful self. Neglect and quarreling are a natural result. Yet, the Spirit is still alive and working: Believers listened to one another's concerns, worked together to solve the problems, and were willing to share the responsibilities. The seven chosen were full of faith, wisdom, and the Holy Spirit. The apostles commissioned the seven. The laying on of hands may have symbolized the transmission of authority—authority the apostles were willing to *share*. The lives of the believers reflected the indwelling Spirit and validated the apostles' teaching. (b) Allow some discussion. Be sure to focus on the positive effects of the Spirit at work: people are concerned with one another's welfare, are willing to listen carefully to one another, are willing to compromise where appropriate and not contrary to God's Word, pray for the Spirit's guidance, submit to the Word of God, and forgive one another as they have been forgiven.

3. Encourage sharing. In this verse Luke uses the word *disciple* for the first time, implying that believers were learning, maturing, becoming like Jesus, and following in His footsteps. The priests mentioned were probably lower priests, who sometimes clashed with the high priests. Nevertheless, it is significant that they were added to the group of believers. (Other progress reports on the growth of the church include 9:31; 12:24; 16:5; 19:20; and 28:31.)

Day 2 • Acts 6:8–15

4. (a) Stephen was a man of faith. He was Spirit-filled. He was blessed by God and full of power, able to perform miracles and wonders. He was wise, articulate, courageous, and forthright. (b) *For personal reflection. Sharing optional.* Welcome participation. Model a response by sharing one characteristic that needs cultivation in your own life. Be very careful, however, not to leave participants with the impression that by trying harder they can get more of the Spirit or get more faith or witness more effectively. Faith, wisdom, courage,

power to witness—all of the gifts of the Holy Spirit are offered to us through Word and Sacrament. Help group members see the importance of "drinking deeply" of these resources.

5. Both Jesus and Stephen were tried before the same court—the Sanhedrin presided over by the high priest (who was most likely the same man, Caiaphas). Each was accused by false witnesses hired by his enemies. A common issue was the destruction of the temple. Neither Jesus nor Stephen jumped to his own defense.

6. (a) The accusations against Stephen centered on his teachings about the temple and the Law. Stephen taught that Christ, not the temple in Jerusalem, was the sign of God's presence among His people. The Jews believed sacrifices could be offered only at the temple and that the Law could never be changed. But Stephen predicted that the temple would pass away and that the Law had given way to the Gospel. (b) All this was threatening to the Jews. It challenged their favorite ideas and offended their national pride. It threatened their identity and position by suggesting that God is not limited to one land and one temple. Stephen's opponents were the unbelieving Grecian Jews from North Africa, Egypt, and the Roman provinces where Tarsus (the home of Paul) and Ephesus (later to become a Christian center) were located. (c) Change comes slowly also in the church. Certainly the Word of God never changes, nor do His Sacraments, the means of grace. Law and Gospel do not change. But certainly church practices may change. Often reevaluation and reassessment are necessary if church practice is to be kept in line with correct teaching. Christians need not fear change that is in line with God's Word and helps to bring about a wider sharing of the Gospel.

Day 3 • Acts 7:1–38

7. (a) God acted through Abraham to establish His covenant with Israel. Through Israel God would send His Son to be the Savior of the world. (b) God acted through Joseph to save His people from famine and to show His faithfulness. (c) God acted through Moses to rescue His people and set them free from bondage.

8. (a) Stephen points out that God's people had many encounters with God: Mesopotamia (7:2); Egypt (7:9); Canaan (7:11); Samaria (7:16); Midian (7:29); and Ara-

bia (7:30). God was not limited to one land; He was present wherever His people were. God did not need the tabernacle or temple since His dwelling is in heaven (7:48–49). (b) God sent His people from Haran to Canaan, from Israel to Egypt and back again. (c) Jealousy (7:9); misunderstanding (7:25); arrogance (7:27); rejection (7:35)—all these the prophets and other spiritual leaders of God's people had to suffer repeatedly.

9. Encourage responses from the group. Point out that human arrogance resists repentance and faith. Feelings of self-satisfaction and self-righteousness do not want to admit sin or see a need for forgiveness and salvation. By nature all people are without true fear and love of God. Only by God's Spirit, working repentance and faith in human hearts, do believers begin to respond to God's will and way. Also, believers still have the old sinful flesh within, which fights against the new creation of the Spirit in human hearts.

10. (a) Ephesians 4:26 urges us to seek resolution right away, before anger has an opportunity to burn its way into our hearts to become enduring resentment or even hatred. (b) 2 Timothy 3:16 urges us to submit our conflict to Scripture, allowing God's Word to teach, rebuke, correct, and train us. (c) James 1:19–20 urges us to listen carefully before we jump to conclusions, perhaps wrongly, and become angry without cause. (d) 1 Peter 4:7–8 urges us to keep our minds clear and in a fit state to pray and to love one another enough to cover over one another's sins with forgiveness.

Day 4 • Acts 7:39–53

11. Stephen accused Israel and the council of resisting God's leaders; of practicing idolatry; of displacing God with the temple; of being stubborn, unbelieving, and deaf to His Word; of persecuting the prophets; of killing His messengers; and of murdering Christ.

12. (a) Allow volunteers to tell of personal experiences. Perhaps some have been confronted by proponents of false religions or sects or have been challenged by self-proclaimed atheists or agnostics. Perhaps some have been tempted to compromise their beliefs in an effort to keep peace in the family or work place. (b) Matthew 10:19–20—Let the Holy Spirit guide your witness and do not worry about coming up with the "right answer." John 14:16–18—Remember that the Holy Spirit lives

within you and will not forsake you. 2 Corinthians 2:17—Speak sincerely, out of your own experiences and convictions. Ephesians 6:18—Pray, asking God to help you, and remember that others are supporting you in their prayers as you are supporting them in your prayers. 1 Peter 3:15–16—Prepare your witness by honoring Christ in your heart; make your witness gently and respectfully.

....

Day 5 • Acts 7:54–60

13. (a) On the surface Stephen's speech and accusations may seem harsh and unrelenting. Yet he was filled with the Holy Spirit and directed his accusers to Jesus. He prayed that God would forgive his killers. It was Stephen's last attempt to reach them. (b) Stephen referred to Jesus as the "Son of Man," a term Jesus Himself seems to have preferred, a term that reflected His link with humanity and also the glorification of His human nature. Stephen's vision, his prayers, and his willingness to risk his life for the sake of the Gospel reflect his intimate relationship with Christ.

14. The texts are all linked with the imminent return of Jesus, the God-man, in judgment on God's enemies. Jesus Himself clearly proved, on the basis of the Scripture they so well knew, that He is God incarnate—their Messiah who took on flesh and blood to be their Savior. Rejecting Him left them nothing but judgment.

15. (a) Share experiences with one another. Tell about times when you've witnessed without speaking a word—when actions and choices have spoken louder than words. Group members may have experienced ridicule or been criticized or shunned. Some may have suffered an economic disadvantage because of their Christian values.

Beware of the human tendency to confuse suffering for the sake of the Gospel with suffering that we bring on ourselves because of our own poor human-relations skills. Also be careful to affirm that it is the Spirit's power living within every Christian that produces a genuine witness. (b) Encourage one another to continue witnessing to God's love in spite of negative reactions. Rejoice together that God keeps His promise not to allow His Word to return empty. Pray together for the Spirit's power to witness effectively.

The Church Takes the Gospel to Samaria and Beyond

Acts 8

Preparing for the Session

Central Focus

Persecution causes Christians to be scattered from Jerusalem into remote areas of Judea and into Samaria (as Christ had said). In those places they courageously and effectively proclaimed the Gospel to Jews, Samaritans, and—in one case—to a visitor from Ethiopia.

Objectives

That participants, led by the Holy Spirit, will

1. be aware of Christ's two mission strategies: bringing people to the Word and bringing the Word to people;

2. recognize that what appears to us to be a setback can actually be meant as a special opportunity to witness for Christ;

3. be alert for special opportunities to share the Gospel with others;

4. be ready to share the Gospel with people without regard to their racial, ethnic, economic, or social background.

Small-Group Discussion Helps

Day 1 • Acts 8:1–3

1. (a) Before His ascension Jesus appeared and gave instructions to the disciples He had chosen (Acts 1:2) and ordered them to wait for the promised gift of the Spirit (Acts 1:4–5). He focused their attention on witnessing for Him and carrying His Gospel to all the world (Acts 1:7–8). Jesus foretold the events that would happen but promised that those who stood firm to the end would be saved and that the Gospel would be preached to all nations before the end of the age comes (Matthew 24:1–14). (b) The Lord's objective is that all

people everywhere will hear the Good News. God loves the world and wants all people to be saved. (c) "You will be My witnesses" (Acts 1:8). The apostles and all believers after them, including every Christian today, are chosen to carry out the Lord's plan. (d) The end of the world will come when the Gospel has been proclaimed to all the world.

2. (a) The believers were scattered throughout Judea and Samaria, just as Jesus predicted. God used persecution for good. (b) Jesus directed the disciples to flee to other areas when persecuted. He promised His witnesses the power of the Holy Spirit to help them when required to testify.

3. Saul (later known as Paul) was born into a strict Jewish home and was educated as a Pharisee, the strictest sect of the Jewish religion. He was very zealous for the law (though ignorant of God's true will in sending Jesus as the Messiah) and persecuted the church. In fact, Saul became the chief agent of the priests, a fanatical extremist who, in striving to outdo even the strictest keeper of the law, would try to stamp out the Christian "heresy" once and for all.

Day 2 • Acts 8:4–13

4. As time permits, let volunteers share their experiences.

5. Listen to the responses of the members of the group. Perhaps believers explained why they had left Jerusalem and moved to the new area. Perhaps they explained why they were willing to suffer loss rather than stop talking about their faith. Perhaps they asked their new neighbors if they had heard of Jesus and then went on to tell all they knew about Him. Perhaps they spoke about the difference Jesus had made in their lives and about the hope and peace they had because of Him. Perhaps they invited their neighbors to confess their sins and be baptized too. They probably discussed Jesus' life, death, and resurrection, and also Pentecost.

6. Philip proclaimed Christ, and people were attentive to Philip's preaching when they saw the miracles he did. They were healed and filled with the joy of faith.

Day 3 • Acts 8:14–17

7. (a) Samaritans intermingled worship of God with worship of pagan idols. (b) Jews regarded Samaritans as being only partly Jewish at best, as unclean (contaminated by the Gentile world and unfit to come into the temple or to engage in Jewish ceremonies and sacrifices), and as holding a warped and incomplete knowledge of the true God. The Samaritans had their own temple and practiced their own sacrifices and worship. They did not regard the entire Old Testament as the Bible, though they shared a belief in the coming Messiah and many other beliefs with the Jews.

8. **Challenge question.** (a) We know that those who heard and believed the Gospel from the Christian refugees received the Holy Spirit within them because no one can acknowledge with faith that Jesus is the Lord without the presence and activity of the Holy Spirit (1 Corinthians 12:3). Furthermore, the Holy Spirit is received by those who are baptized (Acts 2:38). (b) The special outpouring of the Holy Spirit referred to in Acts 8:17 (perhaps evident by the ability to speak in tongues they had not been taught, as in the case of the event described in Acts 10:45–46), made the Spirit's presence obvious and validated the Baptism they had received. Paul speaks of the presence and work of the Spirit in Baptism in 1 Corinthians 12:12–13.

9. The Holy Spirit (a) gave the apostles and other Christians with them the ability to speak in languages they had not learned as an evidence of His presence and power; (b) repeated this sign in the Gentiles who believed the Gospel as a result of Peter's preaching in the house of Cornelius; (c) guides and empowers the church as it forgives or withholds sins as the representative of Jesus; and (d) works through the Gospel in calling people to faith and in sanctifying them.

Day 4 • Acts 8:18–25

10. Simon may have been one of many astrologers of this time. He was powerful and able to control people with his magic, incantations, and spells. Apparently Simon was popular and had influenced the Samaritans for a long time. He was self-important and claimed to be God's representative. Simon was impressed with the visible manifestation of the Spirit, the effects of the lay-ing on of hands. He thought this was magical power and could be bought. He was selfishly motivated, desiring power, and jealous of the control the apostles seemed to have. He wasn't really interested in bringing the Spirit to others.

11. Simon's example warns all who view church membership from a "what's in it for me" perspective. Simon, ironically, achieved the notoriety he craved; his name is linked to "simony," the buying and selling of church offices.

12. When the people in a Samaritan village refused to accept Jesus, John was ready to destroy them with fire. Now he seems less vindictive, more open, eager to preach, call, and persuade.

13. Surely the Gospel had worked in his own heart, and he saw the Samaritans as ripe for harvest, rather than as fuel for fire!

Day 5 • Acts 8:26–40

14. Dramatically these two unlikely people came together under unusual circumstances. God's call through His angel is evidence that this encounter is by God's design. Everything needed is here: an open heart, an inquiring mind, the Word, the Spirit, the water, an eager believer! Racial and class distinctions are ignored. Distractions are few on this lonely desert road. God has put these two particular people together for His purpose.

15. After hearing the Good News about Jesus, the Ethiopian desired Baptism. Philip quickly complied. The Ethiopian became part of the church just as had other converts before him.

16. Surely the Ethiopian understood that the purpose of his conversion was that he might become a witness for Christ. At that time Ethiopia referred to the land south of Egypt called Nubia (Sudan today). Here a very strong Christian church developed. Obviously God used this new convert to bring the Gospel to northern Africa.

17. (a) Encourage participants to tell of times when they were in the right place at the right time to make a witness for Jesus. (b) Encourage participants also to reflect on opportunities God is giving them at this time to be His witness.

The Church Receives an Unlikely Convert

Acts 9:1–31

Preparing for the Session

Central Focus

A dramatic conversion occurs when Saul, on his way to Damascus to arrest Christians and bring them to Jerusalem for punishment, is stopped and overcome by Jesus. Saul repents, is baptized, and is transformed from a persecutor to a preacher of the faith he had come to destroy.

Objectives

That participants, led by the Holy Spirit, will

1. recognize the grace of God in Saul's conversion and enlistment as a missionary;

2. be grateful for God's grace in their own coming to faith in Jesus and in being given a part in His kingdom;

3. more readily forgive and accept those who have sinned against them;

4. rely more consistently on God's grace in their own daily lives.

Small-Group Discussion Helps

Day 1 • Acts 9:1–9

1. Encourage group members to share their sketches of Saul. Your group has already learned something of Saul's earlier life and education in session 6. They have identified him as a strict Pharisee who cruelly persecuted the church, arresting men and women and imprisoning them. Many of these martyrs probably died without a fair trial. In addition, it is helpful to note that he was a choice instrument the Holy Spirit used to bring the Gospel to the Gentiles. While Saul was well versed in Jewish learning, he was also acquainted with the

Greek world and Greek thinking. He spoke Hebrew, Aramaic, and Greek. He was also a Roman citizen from birth and had a sister in Jerusalem with access to the high priestly families (Acts 23:16). Although he was a student, intelligent and learned, he also practiced a trade, was skillful with fabric and was able to make tents, cloaks, awnings, and sails. He was stubborn and uncompromising, a forceful and effective speaker, a born leader who could influence others. Yet he had also a winning disposition and was unselfish.

Perhaps the most important thing to remember about Paul was that everything he wrote about he had received from God and experienced personally. (Sixty percent of Acts focuses on Paul's activities. Half of the New Testament books are his letters.) He wrote and taught what he knew was true because he had received it from Christ Himself—on the Damascus road and in subsequent revelations (Galatians 1:11; Ephesians 3:2–6).

2. What a joy and comfort it is to know how fully Jesus identifies Himself with His people! All believers are part of His mystical body.

3. Jesus might well have accused, condemned, or punished Saul for his sinful persecution and hateful intent. Yet Jesus asked a question instead, with the same loving, pleading tone He used with Martha when He wanted to correct her and show her a better way. Jesus shows His enormous patience in winning sinners. Paul himself writes about God's grace in dealing with him on the Damascus road (1 Corinthians 15:8–11).

4. The proud Pharisee has been humbled. He is blind; he is dependent on his companions, the Sanhedrin police force. He must let them lead him by the hand. His plans are aborted. Now he will be told what to do. Help participants imagine the emotions Saul was experiencing. Perhaps Paul experienced a wide range of human emotions— guilt, a sense of unworthiness, turmoil, despair.

He had to face the reality of what he had done, how wrong and misguided he had been. Surely he confessed to God, admitting his sin and asking for forgiveness. Undoubtedly Saul experienced Jesus' acceptance, grace, and forgiveness personally. (He writes of this so eloquently in his epistles!) Relief must have flooded his soul as he anticipated the next step in God's plans for him.

5. *For personal reflection. Sharing optional.* Share personal experiences. Perhaps an illness, accident, financial setback, divorce, or loss of a job have resulted in changes and a realignment of priorities. Encourage one another to remember that God deals with us for Jesus' sake in love not in anger or vengeance.

Day 2 • Acts 9:10–19

6. God's love and grace are in Ananias's touch. He accepts Saul as his brother in Christ. He affirms Saul's encounter with Jesus. He allows himself to be the instrument of God's healing. He shares the Spirit in Baptism. Ananias has forgiven Saul. He shows mercy to Saul, just as God has shown mercy to him.

7. (a) Perhaps someone in your group is willing to share a personal example of how hard it is to forgive. Our human nature cries for retribution, for justice. Point out that this world deals differently with sin and sinners than Christians do. (b) Central to the Gospel is God's love for sinners—His willingness to sacrifice His own Son to pay for our sins—His willingness to forgive everyone. Only when we ourselves admit our neediness and experience the cleansing mercy of God personally (as Paul did) can we in turn, by the Spirit's power, forgive others. Without forgiveness our witness to the Gospel has a hollow sound. Be sensitive to those in your group who may be withholding forgiveness from others, who may not feel forgiven for something they have done, or who may try to relate to God and others on the basis of justice rather than mercy. Gently guide the discussion so that everyone can see that God calls and uses forgiven sinners to be witnesses for Him.

8. (a) As Jesus stated (Acts 9:15), Paul was called to take the Gospel to the Gentiles (Romans 1:13–14); he was to testify before the rulers of the Gentiles (Acts 25:11–12); and he would proclaim the Gospel to the Jewish leaders (Acts 28:17). (b) Paul suffered for the Lord when he was imprisoned, flogged and beaten, stoned, shipwrecked, and in danger of death. (c) Nevertheless, Christ's power graciously strengthened Paul even in his periods of weakness.

Day 3 • Acts 9:20–22

9. Paul could write and preach eloquently on the grace of God because he had experienced it for himself on the Damascus road. He could write and preach knowledgeably on the Law and the Gospel because he had been a Pharisee, tyrannized and convicted by the Law and liberated by the Gospel. He could write and preach powerfully on the resurrection because he had seen Jesus alive. All his experience living and working within the body of Christ added to his wisdom. When Saul saw Jesus clearly, he began to see others clearly.

10. (a) Paul reports going to Arabia (probably the northern Arabian desert near Damascus) and then, after a period of time, returned to Damascus. Three years after his conversion he returned to Jerusalem, where he spent two weeks with Peter and James. (We learn from Galatians 1:21 and Acts 9:30 that he left Jerusalem for Caesarea and sailed to Tarsus, where he spent 10 years.) (b) Paul may have been 25 years old at the time of his conversion. He had made a drastic about-face. He needed time to reorder his thoughts and grow up as a Christian.

11. Allow group members to speculate about Paul's feelings toward fellow believers. Would he expect them to forgive him? Would he offer to serve with them? Would he try to make amends? Would he cherish and value them as never before? (Note Paul's description of the body of Christ in 1 Corinthians 12:12–31.)

Day 4 • Acts 9:23–25

12. Saul's enemies may have wanted to kill him for the same reason they wanted to kill Stephen. He threatened their religious system. He debated with them, and the Jews couldn't answer him. They couldn't win the argument, so they resorted to violence in an effort to silence the opposition. Again, as with Stephen, Saul preached that, in Jesus, differences of race were eliminated. The Jews might allow Jesus to be preached as the Son of God and even as the Christ, but they could not tolerate the teaching that in Jesus Jews and Gentiles are brothers and sisters.

13. If some group members can tell about a time when the Lord rescued them from danger, encourage them to share this experience. There is one danger from which the Lord has rescued us all—the danger of everlasting

punishment for sin! Jesus took the punishment we sinners deserved. He is the bridge to the Father; He sits at God's right hand and intercedes for us. What comfort we find in knowing that Jesus empathizes with our human condition, that He understands and waits for us with forgiveness.

Day 5 • Acts 9:26–31

14. (a) When Barnabas came to faith he sold a field and shared the profit with his fellow believers. The Holy Spirit was at work. God's message of forgiveness in Christ was proclaimed. God's generosity toward Barnabas was reflected in his generosity toward others. Once again it is clear: The person who has been forgiven much will forgive much. (b) Peter and James surely accepted Saul for the same reasons—they, too, had been accepted and forgiven by God. (c) Too often human nature (our old sinful flesh) dictates otherwise: "I will forgive you if you make up for what you've done . . . if you pay . . . if you change . . . if you meet my specifications." Sometimes, even when a brother or sister has changed, our human nature refuses to acknowledge the change and clings to an accounting of past wrongs. Paul says that the Christian, even one possessing all knowledge and all faith, is still nothing without love. Love is patient, kind, unselfish, constant. Love forgives and forgets. Remind one another that God loves us like that. He doesn't hold our sins against us. (d) Help participants acknowledge that all forgiven sinners who believe in Jesus Christ as Savior are part of the church, Christ's body on earth. Merit does not earn membership. Remind one another also of the believer's continual, daily struggle with sin. Acknowledge our constant need for daily repentance and forgiveness.

15. Encourage volunteers to share their answers to this question.

The Church Affirms Gentile Converts as Equals with Jews

Acts 9:32–10:48

Preparing for the Session

Central Focus

The Lord prepared the church to take the Gospel to the Gentile world by teaching Peter and Jewish Christians that they were no longer to regard Gentiles as unclean but as fully eligible for Baptism and membership in the Christian church.

Objectives

That participants, led by the Holy Spirit, will

1. understand that God accepts into His church on an equal basis people of all races and ethnic backgrounds;

2. earnestly seek to rid themselves of all prejudice and feelings of superiority over people on the basis of gender, economic or social class, or race or ethnic derivation;

3. welcome into the church all those in whom the Holy Spirit works faith through the Gospel.

Small-Group Discussion Helps

Day 1 • Acts 9:32–43

1. (a) Peter was the channel of Christ's power to heal and to restore life. Peter acknowledged that "Jesus Christ heals you" (v. 34). The miracles testified that what the apostles were preaching is the truth. (b) News of the miracles traveled fast.

People undoubtedly asked questions, listened to the apostles' teaching, and believed.

2. (a) Believers are forgiven, cleansed, and covered with Christ's righteousness. Saints do not reflect a righteousness of their own, no matter how good they are, but they reflect the righteousness of Jesus. (b) What a com-

fort to know that our sins are forgiven and that we are holy and righteous before God for the sake of Jesus! What a challenge to live up to that righteousness that is given to us as a gift and to serve God each day, putting sin behind us and yielding to the Spirit, who empowers us to live in that righteousness to which God has called us through the Gospel! "Saint" is an appropriate title for anyone who believes in Jesus as Savior and who, through daily repentance and contrition, is forgiven and strengthened by the Spirit for holy living. The church includes all of us who are at the same time saint and sinner.

3. Lead participants to see that Dorcas's good deeds are not what made her a saint but that her faith in Jesus as her Savior was expressed in loving deeds.

4. **Challenge question.** Old Testament laws prohibited Jews from coming into contact with animals found dead and certainly from eating the flesh of such animals. But these laws did not prohibit Jews from slaughtering clean animals, which would necessarily bring them into contact with the lifeless bodies of the slaughtered animals. Here is another case where the scruples of certain Jews went farther than God's Law did. Peter was coming to see that the ceremonial laws of the Old Testament had been fulfilled and canceled. He was not afraid of being contaminated by contact with a tanner.

Day 2 • Acts 10:1–23a

5. (a) Encourage group members to share their lists of words or phrases describing Cornelius. Cornelius was a God-fearer (a Gentile who worshiped the God of Israel, supported a synagogue, and lived according to the Ten Commandments while not necessarily following the dietary and other ceremonial laws of Judaism). He was devout in prayer (three o'clock was one of the appointed times of prayer for Jews) and was kind, generous, and well respected. He shared his faith openly. In addition, point out that Cornelius was a centurion in the Roman army and commanded a group of about 100 men. Centurions were the backbone of the Roman army. They were required to be good leaders, steady,

prudent, and courageous. Caesarea, 30 miles north of Joppa, was the headquarters of the Roman forces occupying Palestine. Many regiments were composed of Syrian and Samaritan mercenaries, but Cornelius headed a prestigious regiment of Italian soldiers. (b) Both Cornelius and the Ethiopian were God-fearers. Both were devout and eager to learn. Like the centurion in Luke 7:1–10, Cornelius was kind, generous, and believing.

6. (a) Jesus kept dietary laws in perspective. He pointed out that the unclean foods in themselves did not make a person unclean; rather, what was in the heart and expressed itself in sin was what makes anyone unclean—that is, sinful and unacceptable to God. Keeping the dietary laws was a mark of obedience and faith in the God of Israel. In Old Testament times neglect of these laws or failure to keep them was evidence of disobedience and a lack of faith in God. With the coming of Jesus, the Messiah, the dietary laws were fulfilled and canceled. (b) As a well-brought-up Jew, Peter naturally had an aversion to eating anything that God had labeled in the Old Testament as unclean. It was not easy for Peter to put aside a lifetime of attitudes and habits.

7. (a) In Old Testament times God commanded the Jews to keep themselves distinct from their Gentile neighbors. Israel's holiness (apartness from the unbelieving world around them) was to be expressed in all aspects of life. Israel was to be preserved as God's holy people, chosen and set apart to be the instrument through which God would bring forth the Messiah to be the world's Redeemer. But God's intention was always to redeem the entire world and not only Jews. Jews were to be a light to Gentiles, to lead and direct them to God's promise to provide a Savior for all peoples. (b) By showing Peter that God had set aside the dietary laws and had made all foods now clean, God was preparing Peter also to set aside the need to remain separate from Gentiles. Now that the Savior had come, God had made all people clean through forgiveness and righteousness to be received through faith. (c) Peter certainly took some convincing. God repeated the vision and command three times (vv. 11–16). The Spirit prompted Peter to go to Cornelius. The men who came to Peter from Cornelius reported that the angel of God had told Cornelius to invite Peter (v. 22). But Peter caught on. He invited the Gentile messengers into his house and undoubtedly ate with them.

8. *For personal reflection. Sharing optional.* Do not ask participants to answer this question. If some volunteer to comment, however, allow them to do so.

9. Point out that as sinful human beings we often try to accept those who are like us and reject those who do not meet our standards. This sinful self-centeredness leads to prejudice and discrimination that is completely contrary to God's will. The Holy Spirit calls and invites all nations, people, and cultures into His church. The same Spirit works within human hearts, producing love, acceptance, respect, and appreciation of differences. One way the Spirit works is through the Word. Another way is by bringing people together in first-hand, personal contact.

··

Day 3 • Acts 10:23b–33

10. Peter acknowledges that God does not favor one group over another. God loves all people. Jesus is the Savior of the world—not just of Jews. God's mercy and forgiveness through Christ is offered to all sinners regardless of culture or race. Therefore, no one is to reject those whom God accepts.

11. Peter certainly did not want any misunderstanding—whatever Cornelius's intention may have been in falling at Peter's feet. Peter meant to say that he was in no way superior to Cornelius. Like Cornelius Peter was a sinner saved by God's grace. Both stood on an equal footing before God.

12. Cornelius's experience, in which the angel appeared to him and commanded him to send for Peter, certainly corroborated Peter's own experience in which he was commanded to go to Cornelius. The Lord's hand had certainly brought them together, and the Lord was making it clear that Cornelius was to be received into the church on the same basis as the Jews were.

13. Encourage everyone in your group to respond. Note that Cornelius is so open. He is attracted to the religion of the Jews (so culturally different from his own). He is eager to learn, is not arrogant and self-satisfied. He practices his faith openly before Jews, members of his own family, and staff alike. He is ready to listen to instruction he believes comes from God.

14. Again, encourage sharing. Note that, in contrast to Cornelius, Peter is more closed, bound by cultural and

religious conditioning. Peter is more cautious, resistant to change, slower to understand what God is teaching him. Yet, he does listen, and he does learn! Both Peter and Cornelius are learners. LifeLight participants are learners. Explore with your group their role as learners.

Day 4 • Acts 10:34–43

15. Peter admits that he has learned that God accepts all people and that acceptance by God is possible through the work of Jesus Christ to make peace between God and sinners (v. 36). All people are sinners. Jesus made peace with God on behalf of all. Therefore, all people can be at peace with one another. Again emphasize the common need all sinners share. Emphasize the unity all share because all have been redeemed by Christ.

16. The Gentiles in Cornelius's house that day still needed to know of Christ's death and resurrection. They needed to hear the eyewitness accounts of these events. They needed to hear of Christ's return. They needed to know that those who believe in Jesus would be forgiven. They needed the complete Gospel message. These are the main points of Peter's sermon: God's love sent Jesus, who was full of the Spirit. Jesus was compassionate and good. Sinners crucified Jesus. However, His power couldn't be defeated. He rose from death. Jesus is a living presence here and now. We've seen Him. Everyone who believes this is forgiven.

17. (a–c) This is an important section to discuss with your group. Spend some time reflecting on these questions and sharing personal experiences and feelings. Be careful not to foster a we/they or superior/inferior attitude. Emphasize instead the richness of cross-cultural experiences. Everyone benefits. Everyone learns from one another. If your congregation does not reflect cultural diversity, try to determine why. Are there invisible barriers? Especially emphasize the joy that members of Christ's church, His body, experience as they celebrate God's love for everyone.

Day 5 • Acts 10:44–48

18. The Holy Spirit came down on Peter's listeners in visible and audible form. They were gifted with the ability to speak in other languages. Verse 45 says that the Jews who came with Peter could see with their own eyes that the Gentiles had received the Holy Spirit just as they had. This time the Gentiles were given a visible sign of the Spirit's presence, just as the Jews had on the first Pentecost.

19. Perhaps the sign was as much for the benefit of Peter and his friends as it was for the Gentiles. Now they had to realize that the gift of the Spirit put Jews and Gentiles on the same plane. Both are fellow citizens in God's kingdom. God broke down the wall separating the two groups.

20. (a) In Galatians 3:26–29 Paul points out that all who have been baptized are one in Christ Jesus, no matter who they are. This point was made abundantly clear by the Holy Spirit in the house of Cornelius. (b) Our Baptisms tell us that we are one also in Christ Jesus with all other baptized Christians. Gender, economic and social status, race and ethnic background make no difference in this relationship. All of us are God's children through faith in Christ Jesus. All of us are equally loved, valued, and redeemed by God.

21. Encourage sharing. Peter and Cornelius surely shared lodgings and meals. They probably talked, discussed, and learned from each other. Cornelius was probably eager to learn all he could about Jesus from Peter. Peter probably overcame his prejudice against Gentiles. Perhaps they became good friends, now that they were brothers in Christ.

The Church Thrives Despite Persecution

Acts 11–12

Preparing for the Session

Central Focus

The mission to the Gentiles thrives; Peter successfully explains his Baptism of the Gentile Cornelius and his household, and missionaries establish a largely Gentile church in Antioch of Syria. Herod Agrippa I kills the apostle James and tries to kill Peter, but is thwarted and dies.

Objectives

That participants, led by the Holy Spirit, will

1. understand more clearly that God watches over and blesses His church as it goes about His work;

2. feel more confident of God's care and protection in times of danger and crisis;

3. respond more generously to the physical needs of others, especially of other Christians;

4. courageously witness for Christ, trusting God to guide and guard them.

Small-Group Discussion Helps

Day 1 • Acts 11:1–18

1. It is not surprising that the Jewish Christians criticized Peter. They might well have been upset with him for setting aside Old Testament regulations. The fact that Peter received the Gentiles directly into the church through Baptism may have been even more outrageous to them than his eating with Gentiles. Peter's response is calm and cool. Perhaps he realizes that he, too, has had much to learn. He simply explains in detail what happened. He states facts. He doesn't argue or become defensive. He says that he acted at God's direction. He also quotes Jesus' own words. (His six witnesses

strengthened his position also.) Arguing would no doubt have simply led to counter-arguments. Appeals to his own authority would have had no weight when compared to their understanding of the ceremonial law, which they felt Peter had violated. The Word of Jesus spoken to Peter, calmly shared, had a telling effect. What a model also for our discussions and conflict-resolving in the church today!

2. Obviously Luke thought it was important. The Gospel is intended for Jews and Gentiles. Luke wanted to make that perfectly clear. And the point was especially crucial for early Christians, who had to see how Old Testament ceremonial law was fulfilled in Christ.

3. The Spirit was alive in the hearts of those who at first questioned Peter's actions. They were willing to listen to Peter. They trusted his word. They changed their minds. They were reconciled. They rejoiced in the Gentiles' new-found faith. They were not self-serving but were servants of the Word. All this is evidence of the Spirit alive and at work in the Jerusalem church.

4. (a) The controversy was settled peacefully. People were patient with one another, willing to explain and to listen. The temptation to be proud and ambitious and jealous of the status of others was resisted. Instead, love won out. Everyone rejoiced together. (b) Hopefully, participants will have stories to tell. However, differences are not easily resolved. Sometimes we Christians do not realize the power to listen, trust, compromise, love, and forgive that is ours because the Holy Spirit lives within us. Sometimes we react on the level of our sinful human nature and ignore the Spirit that lives within us by faith. You may want to spend some time reading Galatians 5:16–26 together. Reassure one another that our failure to allow the Spirit to direct our lives is sin that has been put to death on the cross with Jesus. Through daily repentance and forgiveness, that sin is erased. We can once again renew our awareness of the Spirit's presence and submit to the Spirit's control.

Day 2 • Acts 11:19–30

5. (a) Barnabas was a good choice because he was "a

good man, full of the Holy Spirit and faith" (v. 24). He was generous (Acts 4:36–37) and big-hearted (9:27), one who was supportive and encouraging to others. He rejoiced with others (11:23) and was quick to give God the glory and credit. He was not jealous. He, like the missionaries to Antioch, came from Cyprus. Barnabas reflects a Christian spirit.

Barnabas was not self-centered but Christ-centered. He could have assumed prominence and power in Antioch, but instead he sought out Saul and worked with him for a year. He was a team player who lived up to his nickname, "Son of Encouragement." (b) In our competitive society people like Barnabas are rare. Yet the church needs more like Barnabas, who are warm and accepting, affirming and encouraging, ready to rejoice in the success of others, unselfish and supportive.

6. Give everyone an opportunity to share how they finished the sentence. Be sure to share how you, too, finished it. Be sensitive to what may be revealed in this sharing. Note similarities in responses. Accept participants' responses. Avoid judging.

7. (a) Discuss ways various groups (especially church groups) respond to human need. Encourage members to tell about their experiences working within these groups. Note what groups are able to do when individuals work together. Ask how decisions are made in the group. Compare what you discuss to the relief fund described in Acts 11:29–30. (b) Take this opportunity to explore ways your LifeLight group might become involved in an appropriate relief effort. You might check with your pastor ahead of time for advice on ideas and procedures.

Day 3 • Acts 12:1–5

8. (a) Herod targeted the apostles. In earlier persecutions the apostles were not singled out. Now they were—especially James, the son of Zebedee and brother of John, whom Herod beheaded just before Passover in A.D. 41. Herod arrested Peter and imprisoned him in the Tower of Antonia at the northwest corner of the temple. (b) Encourage group members to share the human reactions the believers might have felt (discouragement, fear, grief, etc.). Draw from the group how they might feel in a similar situation. Note that the believers had experienced God's blessings in the midst of earlier per-

secutions. (E.g., the Gospel was carried far and wide; congregations grew.) Surely they trusted that God could bless them in the midst of this crisis also. They turned to God in earnest prayer.

9. Peter must have thought about the fact that Jesus had been arrested and killed just before Passover. Perhaps this thought gave him courage and helped him see that he was following his Lord.

10. Share answers to this question. Perhaps God's people simply described what was happening and told Him how they felt. Perhaps they asked God for deliverance and protection and reviewed His faithfulness in the past. Perhaps they expressed their faith and joy in God's power and grace. Note that this is a pattern we see in prayers from the psalms where David seeks refuge in God in times of trouble. Encourage group members to share how they have prayed in similar times.

11. Members who are willing to share their answers should be encouraged to do so. Ask if anyone has been in a situation where his or her life was threatened because of faith. We may not know how we would react in times of extreme crisis. We can trust God's Spirit to work powerfully within us. We can trust His mercy to cover our weakness.

Day 4 • Act 12:6–19

12. (a) The believers were facing an extreme crisis. One apostle had been executed, and a second awaited a similar fate. Who knows what might happen next? The dramatic scene is set. Yet into this setting comes a bit of comic relief. Sleepy Peter must be prodded awake by the angel sent to rescue him. He then groggily stumbles into the street, where he finally comes to his senses. The little hired maid, in her excitement, forgets to unlock the door to let the rescued prisoner safely inside. The skeptical group is amazed that their prayers have been answered so quickly. Relief and joy explode in noisy celebration. The confounded guards are in terror—as well they might be! They receive the execution instead of the prisoner! Herod, the villain, loses the day. (b) All this—dramatic, exciting, thrilling, at times even funny—would make any Christian stand up and cheer in praise of our powerful and gracious God, who defeats evil and wins the victory.

13. Herod ordered four groups of soldiers to guard Peter—one group during each watch of the night. Ordinarily a prisoner was chained by one hand to one hand of his guard. Peter was chained by both hands, with a guard on each side. Two other guards stood at the door.

14. Peter seems totally relaxed. He removed some articles of clothing to get comfortable and was sleeping so soundly he had to be shaken awake by the angel! He seems confident and untroubled by what might happen the next day.

15. (a) Peter finally understands that God has rescued him—that God's power is greater than that of any earthly king—that God's will and plan win out over any who would oppose His church. (b) They are praying—and yet when God answers their prayer, they are slow to believe it. Peter's friends finally understand that God is in control. He answered their prayers. He is the Lord of the church, and they can trust Him. (c) Do not ask for a response to this question.

16. Participants may suggest that the believers praised God, thanked Him, sang hymns, rejoiced together, or reviewed over and over again what had happened.

Day 5 • Acts 12:20–25

17. The spread of God's Word and the growth of the church is phenomenal. It began in Jerusalem with the gift of the Spirit at Pentecost, spread into Judea and Samaria, and was reaching to the ends of the earth, just as Jesus predicted. The Holy Spirit transforms the messengers into powerful witnesses. The Spirit blesses preaching and comes to live within and empower believers for further witness. God Himself breaks down walls between Jew and Gentile, and His grace is offered to the whole world! God turns suffering and persecution into victories that serve His purposes. God builds His church.

18. Encourage everyone in your group to verbalize their commitment to sharing the Gospel with their fellow human beings. Jesus has given this privilege to us—not to angels. Wherever we reflect the love of Christ, in both word and deed, we can be sure that the Spirit is at work. Because someone else shared the Gospel like this, we, too, came to faith. With whom can we share the Good News? Pray together for one another's witness.

19. Ask participants to share what they have gained during this LifeLight course. Encourage them to share how their attitudes and actions have been affected by Bible study. Share your lists of truths you have learned and encouragements you've received. Encourage everyone to enroll in the next LifeLight course and to bring at least one other person with them so that "the word of God" may continue "to increase and spread" (v. 24).